Two-Block Appliqué Quilts

Claudia Olson

Martingale®
& COMPANY

DEDICATION

To my grandmother, Isabel Vincent, and my sister, Pat Peyton. My grandmother inspired me to start stitching, and my sister accompanied me in my sewing while encouraging, entertaining, and motivating me. I dedicate my abilities to the one who gave them to me—God.

Two-Block Appliqué Quilts
© 2004 by Claudia Olson

That Patchwork Place® is an imprint of Martingale & Company®.

Martingale & Company
20205 144th Avenue NE
Woodinville, WA 98072-8478 USA
www.martingale-pub.com

Printed in China
09 08 07 06 05 04   8 7 6 5 4 3 2 1

Library of Congress Cataloging-in-Publication Data

Olson, Claudia.
  Two-block appliqué quilts / Claudia Olson.
     p. cm.
     ISBN 1-56477-574-7
  1. Quilting—Patterns. 2. Appliqué—Patterns.
I. Title.
     TT835.O45 2004
     746.46'041—dc22
                                             2004012856

MISSION STATEMENT

*Dedicated to providing quality products
and service to inspire creativity.*

CREDITS

President ❧ Nancy J. Martin

CEO ❧ Daniel J. Martin

Publisher ❧ Jane Hamada

Editorial Director ❧ Mary V. Green

Managing Editor ❧ Tina Cook

Technical Editor ❧ Karen Costello Soltys

Copy Editor ❧ Liz McGehee

Design Director ❧ Stan Green

Technical Illustrator ❧ Laurel Strand

Nature Illustrator ❧ Claudia Olson

Cover and Text Designer ❧ Regina Girard

Photographer ❧ Brent Kane

Contents

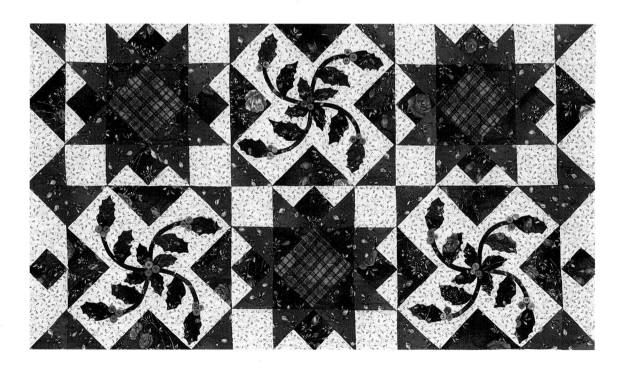

Introduction

Quiet, reflective memories flow around the image of a new spring leaf quivering on the edge of a branch. Sitting quietly at the window of my upstairs room, I spent many childhood hours drawing the leaves and branches that reached toward me. My sketchbooks were filled with pencil and ink drawings of waving, wandering branches and leaves. Occasionally a bird visited, but never stayed long enough to allow a complete portrait. Wanting to add variety to my drawings, I brought home wildflowers, which lasted only slightly longer than the birds' visits. However, the flowers taught me the flowing curves and gentle shadings of turned petals, which would later shape my needlework and appliqué designs. Through my childhood sketches, I learned to re-create nature's shapes on paper while learning about balance and focus.

These memories of quiet moments of concentration are joined with warm memories of sitting by my grandmother's side. She shared fanciful transfer designs with me, which we would press onto fabric with a hot iron and embellish with multicolored threads. The smell of fresh ironing and her sweet perfume, the silkiness of her dress, and the warmth of her arms pervade the memories of my early stitches. Grandma always had time to show me a new embroidery stitch, which I would add to the towel or pillowcase stretched in my hoop. A special way to make the stitches or the correct way to make a French knot was explained slowly and carefully. Concentrated practice sessions were relaxing lessons, where designs took shape and became colorful. Her peaceful patience enveloped me in a seamstress's world that I would retreat to again and again when in need of refreshment.

Discovering appliqué was a fulfilling artistic revelation for me. In this one art form, I could combine my love of drawing with the stitches I enjoyed making. Time spent drawing a new design could now be paired with gratifying hours of stitching the shapes onto a background fabric. The leaves that I remembered from my drawings took on new textures and colors. I could finally complete those elusive birds by working from photographs. Other animals were soon added to my pictures. But, unlike the birds, which seemed safe on their branches surrounded by leaves, the animals seemed to lack the right setting.

I looked for piecing that would frame an animal in a way that would suggest a house or a den. I found blocks that had an open space just waiting for an appliqué design, and found ways to create new appliqué space within pieced blocks. When a friend asked for a pieced quilt with animal appliqués, I enthusiastically transferred my animal creations to pieced blocks in a quilt setting made just for her. Thus, *Two-Block Appliqué Quilts* was begun.

Appliqué Spaces in Pieced Blocks

Most appliqué designs seem to be stitched onto blocks that are made of one square of fabric. They usually contain little or no actual piecing, other than perhaps a sashing strip that acts as a frame around the appliqué design. While such settings are attractive and can be restful to the eye, they lack geometric interest. By working with a two-block format, I find that I can design a space suitable for appliqué elements and at the same time create geometric interaction between the two blocks.

Blocks that work well in a two-block pieced quilt design fit together like puzzle pieces. The lines of the pieces flow in an unbroken fashion from block to block. Sometimes the pieces of the blocks form a secondary pattern by extending the design of one block into the next. When a secondary pattern is formed, I often continue the pattern into the border for a finished look.

For a successful two-block appliqué quilt, you need to meet the same criteria as for pieced block combinations while also making spaces for appliqué. Often a natural space is available within one of the two blocks. In "Crossed Stars" (page 50), an appliqué space exists in the Double Cross block. Following a Christmas theme, holly leaves and berries weave across the crossed white spaces.

Other blocks may provide large appliqué spaces if the center part of the block is replaced by a piece of background fabric. For instance, the Garden Path block can be simplified by eliminating all of the small four patches and the center triangles. When you take a look at "Crow's Path" (page 57) and "Gentleman's Garden" (page 90), you'll see that the revised Garden Path block looks like an on-point square that is filled with appliquéd flowers or wild animals. Allowing the appliqué to extend beyond the confines of the background square lets the appliqué meld creatively into the pieced area of the quilt.

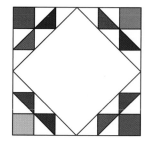

Garden Path Block   Garden Path Variation Block

In "Interlocked Mosaic Stars" (page 101), I took the crossed arrows out of the center of the Interlocked Mosaic Arrows blocks to provide appliqué space.

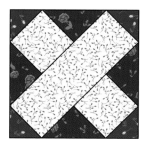

Double Cross Block

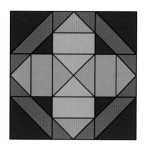
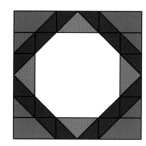

Interlocked Mosaic Arrows Block   Interlocked Mosaic Block

Another example of modifying a block to allow space for appliqué is in "Folk-Art Stars" (page 79). This time, I eliminated the center patch of a Corn and Beans block to make a new Mosaic variation. The center of this new block is used to house creatures and garden tools. I also changed the color value of the outside triangles, using lighter ones to encircle a single ring of dark triangles to frame the appliqué. To help the viewer focus on the appliqué rather than the piecing, I chose light colors for the accompanying Ohio Star blocks.

 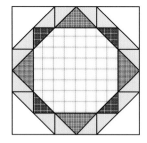

Corn and Beans Block   Mosaic Variation Block

While one of the blocks of "Azalea Album" (page 42) provided a ready-made appliqué space, I noticed that more space would be available if I changed the color value of some of the block corners. By substituting white fabric for the print fabric, a new appliqué space appeared when the blocks were joined.

Lighthouse Beacon
Block   Album Block

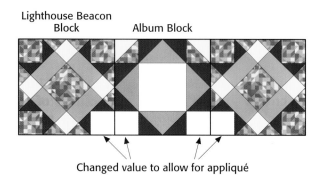

Changed value to allow for appliqué

"No Squirrels Allowed" (page 112) required new techniques that would open even greater areas of the quilt for appliqué. I chose the Arrow Points block for this quilt, using darker colors and all of the piecing detail in the corners of the quilt. As I progressed toward the quilt center, I replaced some patches with the lighter background fabric, and in the centermost blocks I substituted some of the intricate piecing with simpler piecing and larger patches of background fabric. Long appliquéd branches with birds, leaves, and even a squirrel take the place of whole patchwork blocks. The use of lighter colors and less-complicated piecing at the center of the quilt helps the viewer focus on the creatures in the tree without the interference of piecing and seam lines.

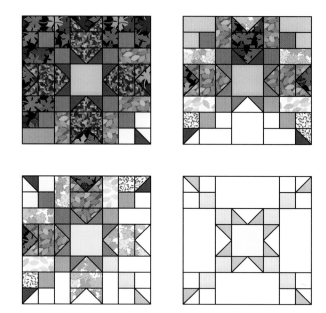

Arrow Points Block and Variations

Try playing with the following designs to start your own creative process and notice aspects that make the block combinations work. Watch for new ways to make spaces for appliqué designs. Also, notice how the alterations made in blocks allow the lines to flow and help the viewer's focus to change.

For instance, if we replace the dark center triangles and square of a Pine Burr block with background fabric, we create a new appliqué space. We can combine the revised Pine Burr block with a Mosaic Star or Federal Square block for a workable combination. Both of these alternate pieced blocks have diagonal corner treatments that allow the lines to flow smoothly from them to the Pine Burr block. In a sample layout of Pine Burr and Federal Square blocks, notice that the appliqué space has a diagonal frame.

In another example, let's start with the Town Square block. When we replace the dark squares in the center of the block with light ones, an appliqué area framed by triangles and corner squares remains.

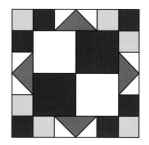

Town Square Block   Town Square Variation

Pine Burr Block

We can now pair this block variation with other pieced blocks for different effects. Paired with a Thrifty Squares block, a stepping-stone pattern emerges in the quilt.

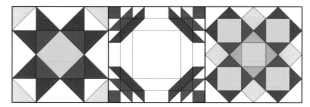

Mosaic Star Block   Pine Burr Variation   Federal Square Block

Pine Burr Variation and Federal Square Quilt Layout

Town Square Variation and Thrifty Squares Quilt Layout

If we replace Thrifty Squares with the Broken Wheel block, the two-block design generates a feeling of curved lines. Using a block combination with connecting or parallel diagonal lines is usually the best choice for a two-block quilt since it creates greater geometric interest.

For an entirely different look, we can simply change the outer triangle fabrics in Town Square and swap the dark and light color placement in parts of Broken Wheel to draw more attention to the appliqué. Such recoloring not only changes the focus, but also adds more appliqué space while creating a dark, secondary star in the quilt layout.

Broken Wheel Block

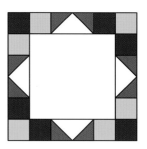

Town Square Variation Recolored

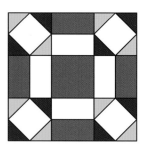

Broken Wheel Recolored

Broken Wheel and Town Square Variation Quilt Layout

Recolored Quilt Layout

Let's take a look at one more example of how revising a complex pieced block can give you an interesting block with plenty of space for appliqué. The Beacon Lights block offers a square in its center that is on point. We can lighten the center square and pair it with either a Broken Dishes or a Washington Pavement block for an interesting quilt setting. Using traditional coloring and pairing Beacon Lights with Broken Dishes gives the quilt a light, airy feeling.

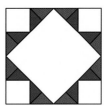

Beacon Lights Block

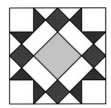

Broken Dishes Block Beacon Lights Variation #1 Washington Pavement Block

Beacon Lights Variation #1 and Broken Dishes Quilt Layout

Let's replace the dark inner squares in the Beacon Lights block with light ones to make more appliqué space. At the same time, we can replace the plain corner triangles on the Washington Pavement block with pieced units. By using darker colors in these units and in the outer triangles of the Beacon Lights block, the blocks look much more solidly connected in the quilt layout. Using the dark outside triangles changes the focus from the pieced blocks to the appliqué space.

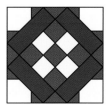

Beacon Lights Variation #2 Washington Pavement Variation

Beacon Lights Variation #2 and Washington Pavement Variation Quilt Layout

Creating appliqué spaces in pieced blocks can be challenging and fun. Experiment with blocks that provide a central open square after pieces are replaced with simpler piecing or lighter fabrics. For an alternate block, choose a complementary one with lines that flow toward the primary block. Remember to color blocks in such a way that the appliqué will be enhanced and the piecing will not dominate in intensity or pattern.

Materials and Supplies

Materials chosen for appliqué—from the fabrics to the types of tools and supplies you use—should be functional and easy to work with. Some of the tools mentioned in this chapter may make your stitching easier and help you enjoy the appliqué process more. Try the various tools with the different techniques presented to see which you prefer.

choice since it may discolor surrounding fabrics when your finished quilt is washed.

Vary the prints within each color range to add interest to your appliqué.

FABRICS

Choose 100%-cotton fabric that is smooth and tightly woven. Check the threads by touch and sight; fabric that is woven with thick, lumpy thread is unsuitable for appliqué because it will not provide a crisp edge when turned under. It may also fray easily along the edges. You want to select fabric that can withstand handling while hand sewing.

You'll also need to choose a variety of prints for appliquéd flowers and animals so you can easily distinguish the individual pieces. Mottled, marbled, batik, and tone-on-tone prints work well for appliquéd flowers. Add feathered, fur-look, or natural textured prints to your fabric stash for appliqué animals and birds.

Prewash your fabric with a small amount of soap or detergent in a white sink or plastic basin. Rinse the fabric repeatedly to remove any extra dye. A fabric that colors your white sink or basin may be a poor

THREADS AND THREAD FINISHES

I prefer to use 100%-cotton thread for all of my appliqué. Since my fabrics are made of cotton, the 100%-cotton thread will hide between the fibers of the fabric better than poly-wrapped cotton thread. It is also less prone to knotting and is smoother to work with. Cotton thread thickness varies, so you may want to test available brands to discover which ones you prefer. Vintage mercerized cotton thread can also be of good quality and it's fun to look for these old spools of thread at yard and estate sales. For basting shapes, choose lightweight, white cotton thread. Dark thread could leave colored spots on light fabrics.

Silk thread is also nice to work with because it is extremely smooth and comes in a wide array of colors. Keep silk thread length short, however, because the more times it is pulled through the fabric the more likely it is to knot and fray.

Embroidery floss or pearl cotton can be used to embellish appliqué shapes. You can reduce tangling, thinning, and fraying by using a thread conditioner on your appliqué threads. A thread conditioner, such as Thread Heaven, creates a smooth finish on the thread that makes it slide easily through fabric and leaves no residue. Knot the end of the thread that you just cut nearest to the spool to further reduce tangles.

I recommend using two strands of embroidery floss for fine-detail embellishing. For a little more dimension, use size 8 pearl cotton, which is easy to work with and gives a more raised texture than floss. For a chunkier look when outlining folk-art shapes in buttonhole stitches, try using size 5 pearl cotton.

NEEDLES AND PINS

Most appliqué artists favor a size 10 or 11 Sharp or a straw needle for precise sewing. I prefer a size 11 Sharp because the length is similar to that of a regular sewing needle; straw needles are a bit longer and thinner. Sharps or straw needles can also be used for basting.

When embellishing with floss, switch to a large-eye embroidery needle for easier threading. For quilting, I prefer size 10 or 12 Between needles, which (for me) require a magnifying glass to thread, but allow me to make very small quilting stitches. I use silk pins when positioning my appliqués because they are very fine and sharp, but I only use them until my shapes are basted in place because they have a tendency to capture and snag my sewing thread. I find that basting lets me position an appliqué piece more accurately than pinning.

THIMBLES

Thimbles come in a variety of styles and materials. I prefer a metal thimble with a raised lip that prevents the needle from slipping. Since wearing a thimble takes time to get used to, experiment with a few types to find the one that best suits you. After finding a thimble that you like, you most likely won't want to sew without one.

SCISSORS

Use small, pointed scissors to easily cut appliqué pieces and threads. Large scissors make trimming around templates more difficult and less accurate. Also, small scissors are finely sharpened to the tips, allowing snipping up to a precise thread on deeply indented curves. Switch to utility scissors to cut out plastic and freezer-paper templates.

MARKING TOOLS

The variety of available marking implements can confound any quilter. Look for a type of pencil that is free from oil and graphite (lead), or choose a chalk pencil. Use white pencils or slivers of white soap to mark dark fabrics. Light fabric can be marked with gray pencils designed specifically for quilting. A No. 2 pencil or a fine-lined mechanical pencil can be used when marking background fabric if you draw inside the actual appliqué lines. When marking, use light lines and try removing them from a test piece of fabric before marking your project. Quilters' pencils usually erase more easily than common No. 2 pencils.

When it comes to marking tools, a few warnings are in order. Colored chalk can be extremely difficult to remove from fabric and may require scrubbing with soap. Disappearing pens require washing with soap to completely remove the ink, and the chemicals have been known to permanently discolor fabric. Use pencil or permanent-ink markers to label template plastic, but allow the markings to dry completely before using the templates on fabric. Washable ink may rub off onto your ironing board or appliqué fabrics.

SKEWERS AND BRUSHES

Turning under the seam allowance of shapes for needle-turn appliqué is easier to do with a stick. I use a bamboo skewer cut to the length of a pencil. Because it has more friction than a needle, the bamboo will stick better to the fabric and make it easier for you to push under the fabric. The skewer is also useful for holding the seam allowance of a small shape to the back side while pressing, since it keeps tender fingers away from the hot iron.

A paintbrush is necessary when using the fabric-starch appliqué method. Pressing shapes with fabric starch is best accomplished on a semihard board rather than a soft ironing board. I made a small pressing board from a scrap of wood covered with one layer of cotton batting and cotton fabric. This way, my ironing board cover is preserved, since over time, multiple applications of fabric starch can stain. Test fabric starch on prospective fabrics to make sure that they will not be damaged. The starch is diluted for the appliqué method and should be applied in a thin line to the seam allowance only, not to the front of the appliqué piece.

BIAS BARS

Bias bars are used for making stems in floral appliqué. They enable you to make yards and yards of stems and vines, if necessary, all with a consistently even width.

Bias bars are made either of nylon or metal, and they range in width from ⅛" to ½". Nylon bars are cooler to the touch and prevent burned fingers, but metal bars give a crisper pressed edge.

TWEEZERS

Tweezers are used for several tasks while appliquéing. They are used to pull freezer paper out from under a nearly finished shape. Small basting stitches are easily removed with a quick pull from tweezers. Also, tweezers are handy for tucking a darker fabric under a flower petal to give the appearance of a turned petal.

TEMPLATE PLASTIC AND FREEZER PAPER

Template plastic should be heat-resistant and able to withstand multiple ironings if you are going to use the fabric-starch appliqué method described on page 15. I recommend Templar because it is sturdy and will last through pressing an entire project. It is a heat-resistant plastic with a shiny side and a dull side. The dull side can be written on for labeling purposes.

Freezer paper, in my opinion, is the best material for tracing appliqué patterns since it sticks to the fabric with a quick pressing. (Trace onto the dull paper side and the shiny side adheres to the fabric.) Also, freezer-paper templates can be used several times, as long as they still stick to the fabric. Freezer paper comes on a large roll and can be found at most grocery stores.

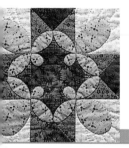

Appliqué Techniques

There seem to be as many variations of appliqué as there are quilters. The most common comment that I have heard from beginners is that they wish someone would show more methods than needle-turn appliqué, which they find too difficult. Thus, I present to you the three most popular methods of appliqué and have listed the most commonly followed practices used for each method. Choose the method that best suits your comfort level and adapt it to your favorite sewing techniques.

All of the following appliqué methods start with these five steps.

1. Prewash fabric to rinse out any color that will run. Press fabric.
2. Cut the background square 2" longer and wider than what the finished size will be and serge or turn under the edges to prevent fraying during hand sewing. When the block has been completed, trim the excess fabric before setting the square into its block.

3. Darken the lines on your paper pattern for easy viewing when tracing. Mark the top of the pattern with pencil and the top of the fabric square with a thread so you can easily line them up in the same direction.
4. Make templates from your paper pattern by tracing each pattern piece onto the dull side of template plastic. Label the templates with the appropriate piece numbers.
5. Using a light box, mark placement lines on the background fabric with a light pencil line. Draw all shapes slightly smaller than the actual size of the piece so the appliqué pieces will cover your markings.

FREEZER-PAPER APPLIQUÉ

Freezer-paper appliqué is a good choice if you want a firm edge against which to fold the fabric edges. When freezer paper is used behind the fabric piece, there is no question about where to turn the fabric. When appliquéing layered shapes, most quilters choose to sew one piece at a time to the background block, layering as they go. If that is your choice, follow "Layered Freezer Paper," below. If you wish to assemble your flower or animal or other figure before sewing it to the background, follow "Preassembled Freezer-Paper Shapes" on page 14.

Layered Freezer Paper

1. Trace the reverse image of the finished appliqué shapes onto freezer paper by tracing around your plastic templates. Make dashed lines along the edges that will be covered by other appliqué shapes and therefore will not need to be turned under.
2. Label the paper pieces with the piece number. You might also find it handy to include the pattern name.
3. Cut out the traced paper pieces, cutting exactly on the drawn lines.
4. Press the shiny side of the paper pieces to the wrong side of the fabrics, using a dry iron set on "wool." The cotton setting may be too hot and can discolor fabric or make it shiny. The wool setting will be hot enough to soften the wax coating so that it adheres the paper to the fabric.
5. Trim the fabric around each paper shape, leaving a scant ¼" seam allowance. Clip sharply indented curves, stopping two or three threads before the paper edge.

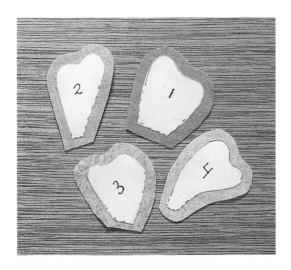

Leave a scant ¼" seam allowance around each freezer-paper template.

6. Fold the raw edges of the fabric over the edge of the paper and baste the fabric in place with cotton basting thread. Leave excess thread attached for later use.

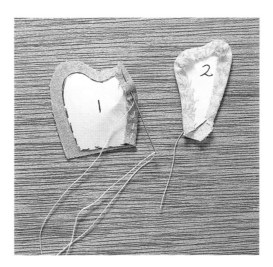

Fold the seam allowances firmly over the edges of the freezer paper and baste in place.

7. Position prepared shape 1 on the background fabric and baste it in place using the thread tail remaining from step 6. For precise positioning, place the pattern and fabric on a light table. Tape all edges of the pattern and fabric to the light table and trace inside the pattern lines. If you don't have a light table, try tracing the design onto a clear plastic overlay sheet with a permanent marker. Lay the plastic over the background fabric, taping it in place along the top edge. Using tweezers, place the appliqué shapes in position beneath the plastic. Baste in place in the same manner.
8. Select thread that matches the piece to be appliquéd and blindstitch the shape in place. If the piece has an edge that will be covered by another appliqué piece, begin and end sewing at opposite sides of the edge that hasn't been turned under. If the shape will be stitched around all edges, stitch nearly all the way around the shape, stopping about ¾" from the point where you started. See "Beginnings to Endings" on page 16 to make small, hidden blind stitches.

9. Clip and remove all basting threads, taking care not to clip your appliqué thread. Remove the freezer paper with tweezers. Finish stitching the shape in place.

Gently tug the freezer paper with tweezers to remove it.

10. If more pieces are to be appliquéd on top of the first piece, position shape 2 over shape 1. Repeat steps 8 and 9 to stitch the new piece and all remaining pieces in place.

Preassembled Freezer-Paper Shapes

1. Follow steps 1–6 of "Layered Freezer Paper" on page 13.
2. Layer the appliqué pieces directly over the paper pattern, pinning them together to form a unit.
3. Baste the pieces together and remove the pins. If a dark fabric shape, such as a leaf or the back side of a petal, needs to be tucked under an assembled flower, insert this piece last. Tuck it under the assembled flower and baste it in place. See "Tips and Tricks" on page 18 to make a turned petal.

Baste the pieces together to form a single unit to be appliquéd.

4. Blindstitch the shapes together where they overlap, matching the thread color to each shape.

Blindstitch the shapes together where they overlap.

5. Snip the basting stitches from the edges that have been sewn and turn the appliqué unit to the back side. Cut away the freezer paper up to the edges that are sewn, being careful to avoid cutting the fabric.

Cut away interior portions of basting stitches and freezer paper so that you'll be able to easily remove the paper when appliqué is complete.

6. Sew on any remaining appliqué pieces, such as flower centers, and embroider desired embellishments.

Embroidered stamens add lifelike interest to flowers.

7. Baste the assembled unit to the background fabric. Blindstitch it into place. As you near the end of each appliqué section, snip the basting threads and pull out the freezer paper. If you reach a piece that is colored differently, finish off your first thread color as described in "Beginnings to Endings" on page 16, and change the thread color.

After basting the unit to the background fabric, appliqué the edges in place.

FABRIC-STARCH APPLIQUÉ

Fabric-starch appliqué allows you to turn under fabric edges at the ironing board before sewing. It produces a crisp, pressed edge around shapes while eliminating the need for basting. You'll need a few extra supplies for this method, including a paintbrush, a small dish, spray fabric starch, a wooden skewer, and heat-resistant template plastic, such as Templar.

1. Trace each shape onto the dull side of template plastic, cut out the shapes on the drawn lines, and label the templates.
2. Use your templates to trace the patterns onto freezer paper as described in "Layered Freezer Paper," steps 1–5, on page 13. Remove the freezer paper.
3. Mix a solution of about 80% to 90% spray starch and 10% to 20% water in a small dish.
4. Place a cutout appliqué shape on your pressing board and, holding the plastic template in place, use a small paintbrush to paint the seam allowance of the shape with the starch solution.

Dab seam allowances with spray-starch solution.

5. Holding the plastic template in place with a wooden skewer to prevent burned fingers, carefully press the edges of the fabric over the template edges with a dry iron on the wool setting. A cotton setting may curl the plastic, discolor the fabric, or make the fabric shiny. Press until the fabric is dry and the edge is set.

Press the seam allowance firmly over the edge of the plastic template.

6. Appliqué the shapes in place as described in "Layered Freezer Paper," steps 7–10.

NEEDLE-TURN APPLIQUÉ

Needle-turn appliqué is a method chosen by appliqué artists who prefer to turn pieces under as they appliqué, rather than baste or press them under first. Since the firm edge of freezer paper is absent, it is sometimes harder to get an exact duplicate of a shape. With this method, the quilter turns or tucks under the seam allowance of each appliqué shape before appliquéing each section of the design. I find that using a wooden skewer to turn under the edges works better than using a needle, which slips more than the skewer.

1. Trace the appliqué patterns onto the template plastic, freezer paper, or cardboard to make a template of each shape. Do not reverse the image for this method. Label each template with the shape number.
2. Cut out the templates, cutting exactly on the drawn line.
3. Draw a line around the templates onto the right side of the fabric with a white or gray chalk pencil. If using freezer paper, you can iron the pattern pieces to the right side of the fabric to use as a turn-under guide.

4. Cut out the appliqué shapes, leaving a scant ¼" seam allowance around the marked lines.

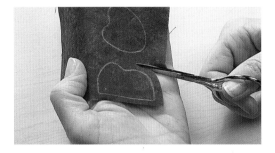

Cut a scant ¼" outside each appliqué shape.

5. Pin and then baste the appliqué pieces to the background fabric. Remember to baste more than ¼" inside the edges so that you have space to turn under the seam allowance.
6. Select thread that matches the piece to be appliquéd and blindstitch the shape into place. If the piece has an edge that will be covered by another shape and will therefore not be turned under, begin and end sewing at opposite sides of the edge that won't be turned under. (The section that will be overlapped by another shape won't be stitched in place.) Tuck under the seam allowance using the point of a wooden skewer just before sewing down an edge. You don't need to turn under the entire edge at once; turn under about ½" ahead of your stitching at a time. See "Beginnings to Endings" at right to make small, hidden blind stitches.

Turn under only a short distance of the seam allowance at a time and stitch in place.

7. If more pieces are to be appliquéd on top of the first piece, position shape 2 over shape 1. Repeat steps 5 and 6 to stitch the new piece as well as all remaining pieces.

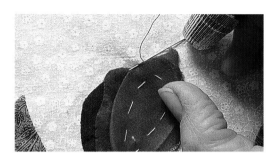

Appliqué additional shapes, working from the bottommost to the topmost piece.

COMBINATION TECHNIQUES

Many appliqué artists choose to combine appliqué methods to achieve nicely shaped and sized pieces. I have met several quilters who cut freezer-paper templates and press them onto the right side of the fabric. Then, they needle turn their pieces and use the freezer paper as a guide. Other quilters cut reverse-facing freezer-paper templates, press them onto the reverse side of the fabric, and then use fabric starch to turn under seam allowances. Like the traditional freezer-paper method, the freezer paper is removed just before the stitching is finished.

BEGINNINGS TO ENDINGS: PERFECTING THE APPLIQUÉ STITCH

Cut thread by making a diagonal snip. Thread length should be about as long as your forearm. Keeping the thread short will help prevent it from knotting and breaking. You may find it easier to thread the needle if you wet both the eye of the needle and the tip of the thread; this prevents static repulsion. Knot the end of the thread last snipped from the spool to keep it winding in the right direction. (Left-handed quilters should knot the opposite end of the thread.)

1. To make a knot, wind the end of the thread around the needle two or three times. Then, slide the knot down to the end of the thread. Finally, I recommend sliding the thread across a thread

conditioner to help it glide more easily through the fabric.

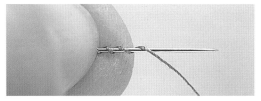

Wrap thread twice around the needle, and then slip the wraps to the end of the thread to knot.

2. Begin sewing by hiding the knot behind your appliqué shape. Slip the needle beneath the shape to be appliquéd and push it behind the seam allowance, coming out at the fold.

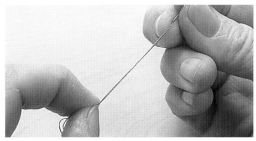

Hide the knot by slipping needle through the folded edge of fabric.

3. Make the first stitch by poking the needle down through the background fabric directly beneath the area where the thread comes out of the shape.

Stitch into the background fabric directly below where the thread exited the appliqué shape.

4. Push the needle back up through the background fabric a short distance away and stab it up through the folded edge of the shape.

Take a tiny stitch, coming back up through the folded edge of the appliqué.

5. Continue in the same fashion, making blind stitches that are small and even. As you approach the next bit to be stitched, if the fabric appears puckered or bumpy, tuck it under or smooth it out with your skewer before stitching it in place.

   While stitching, take a few precautions to avoid breaking or knotting the thread. Each time the thread is pulled through the fabric it receives wear at the place that rubs against the eye, and thread can easily thin, fray, or even break. To prevent thinning, occasionally move the needle to a new position along the thread. After the third or fourth move of the needle, drop the thread to allow it to untwist to prevent knots. Also keep your eye on the loose end of the thread and snip it when it starts to look tattered. It will begin to look like a fuzzy split end, which can easily wrap around the long thread and form a knot.

6. When you reach the point where the stitching began, rotate your project and take two or three backstitches. Then, turn your project to the back side. Make three or four small stitches on the back, behind the seam allowance of the appliqué shape, stitching through the background fabric only. Then, cut your thread. You have successfully completed sewing your shape in place!

A few tiny backstitches secure the thread without the bulk of a knot.

TIPS AND TRICKS

Making some types of shapes may require a technique that is not explained in the general appliqué instructions. To ensure your success, for these particular shapes, I'll show you ways to appliqué them with excellent results. Some of these shapes are used repeatedly in floral appliqué, so you'll find yourself using the following tips quite frequently.

Stems and Branches

Narrow stems can be a frustration to a new quilter if only needle-turn techniques are used. I have found the bias-bar method to be very simple and effective for making and appliquéing stems.

Cut 45° bias strips that are the width of the finished stem size plus ⅞". Fold the strip in half lengthwise with wrong sides together and then sew a scant ¼" seam. Trim the seam allowance to ⅛". Insert the appropriate-sized bias bar into the sewn fabric tube and twist the fabric until the seam lies along one flat side of the bar. Press the seam flat, pressing on both sides of the bar to set a crisp edge. Slip the bar out of the fabric and press again. Cut the long stem piece into sections long enough to tuck behind another appliqué shape and blindstitch them into place.

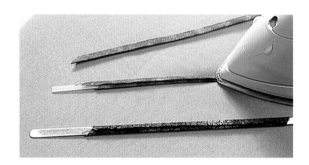

Bias bars make quick and accurate work of stem preparation.

When making branches for "No Squirrels Allowed" (page 112), I cut bias strips the width of the largest branch size plus ⅞". Follow the above directions, except make the seam larger as your stitching nears the end of the strip, until the branch size is almost ¼" wide. Trim the seam as described above and press the bias tube, using decreasing sizes of bias bars to fit the width of the tube.

Light-Colored Appliqué Pieces

A previously appliquéd piece or the background fabric may show through light-colored appliqué pieces. To avoid this situation, cut a piece of interfacing slightly smaller than the shape to be appliquéd. Place the interfacing behind the shape and appliqué the piece in place. Fusible interfacing works great for this situation. If your fusible interfacing has enough body, you can use it in place of freezer paper, simply turning under the appliqué edges along the edge of the interfacing. Note the photograph following step 1 on the opposite page—it shows the wrong side of a squirrel whose white belly has interfacing attached.

Flower Petals

Unlike real flowers, many appliquéd flower petals don't need to be made as full petals. Because the petals overlap, you can't see the entire petal, so you don't need to appliqué all of it. For instance, if petal 1 is to be mostly covered by petal 2, you need only to make a partial petal 1. You'll have less to stitch and less bulk in the finished block.

Also, pieces that are covered by another shape do not need to be stitched in place where they will be overlapped, which makes it easy to remove freezer-paper templates. Remember to include a ¼" seam allowance on these edges, even though they won't be turned under. It will give you enough fabric to tuck beneath the overlapping piece.

Turned Petals

In appliqué, to indicate that the underside of a petal is showing, make a darker piece for underneath by cutting a circle of fabric with a diameter ½" longer than the edge of the petal it is to go under. Turn under about ¼" along one edge of the circle (so it looks like a flat tire), then fold under the same amount on the opposite edge. Fold the entire circle in half, bringing the two remaining curved edges together. Press.

Clever folding of a circle makes a perfect underside for a flower petal.

Tuck the dark piece under a concave flower-petal edge so that its outer edge covers the markings on the background fabric, and appliqué it in place with matching thread. Finish sewing the petal in place.

*Tuck the folded circle in place
with the help of tweezers.*

Circles

Circles are perhaps the easiest shape to sew because it's easy to get a perfectly turned-under curved edge with the help of some basting. I use freezer paper cut to the finished size of the circle and press it to the wrong side of the appliqué fabric. Cut the fabric a scant ¼" outside the freezer-paper edge. Keeping the circle flat, sew a running stitch about ⅛" away from the edge of the seam allowance. Next, place a cardboard or plastic template the same size as the freezer-paper template on top of the freezer-paper circle. Pull the thread gently to draw the seam allowance over the edge of the template. Press to set a crisp edge. Loosen the gathers slightly to remove the templates (freezer paper and cardboard or plastic), adjust the gathers back in place, and re-press the edge. Appliqué the circle in place as you would any other shape.

*Pull gathers to tighten the seam allowance
over the circle templates and press.*

Leaves

Pointed leaves are made in different ways, depending upon the appliqué technique used.

If using freezer paper, first fold the pointed end of the leaf fabric over the point of the paper.

Fold the point over the freezer paper first.

Then, fold one side of the leaf over the paper and press or baste it in place.

*Next, fold one edge over the
point and baste in place.*

Finally, fold the other side of the leaf over the paper and baste.

*Fold the second edge over
the point and continue basting.*

For needle-turn appliqué, begin stitching along one side of the leaf because it's always easiest with needle turn to start along a straight or nearly straight edge. Use your skewer to turn under the fabric edge as the point comes in view.

As you approach the tip of the leaf, use a skewer to turn under the fabric all the way past the marked point.

Tuck under the side of the leaf completely up to the leaf point, where you'll take a final stitch straight down through the background fabric.

Take a stitch directly at the leaf point to secure a sharp point.

Then, tuck under the other side of the leaf point with the skewer and stitch in place. You may find that there is excess fabric to be tucked under on the second side of the point. If so, trim the seam allowance so the point won't be so lumpy.

Sweep the seam allowance under on the other side of the point and continue stitching.

If your leaf point does not look as pointed as you would like, create a new, better point with thread. Starting at the end of the leaf, add a stitch on each side of the fabric point with your appliqué thread. Fill in with more stitches, if needed, to give your new thread point some substance.

EMBELLISHING

Embellishing with embroidery and Pigma pens can give your finished appliqué piece definition, shape, and interest. For instance, when Terry Vaughn made "Gentleman's Garden" (page 90), she shaded the flower petals with a Pigma pen to make them look curved. She also added more shading to the flower centers to darken the fabric. To complete the details, she embroidered the stamens using a stem stitch.

The flower centers of "Azalea Album" (page 42), made by Sandy Ashbrook, and "Interlocked Mosaic Stars" (page 101), made by Linda Riesterer, are both embroidered. Sandy and Linda used a stem stitch and French knots in gold and yellow threads to add sparkle and definition to the flower centers.

Animals with small parts can be a challenge to appliqué. Embroidery can help define an edge, add detail, or provide texture. I outlined the edge of the squirrel's white stomach in "No Squirrels Allowed" (page 112) with a stem stitch to define and separate it from the background fabric. I embroidered the birds' feet, too small to make in fabric, with a chain stitch. A satin stitch is perfect for the birds' eyes and beaks.

Embroidery stitches are also a good way to create furlike texture, as shown on the animals in "Crow's Path" (page 57). The animals' legs are outlined with stem stitch. Also, several animals, such as the fox and elk, have small patches of white fur that were made using pearl cotton and the satin stitch.

In "Folk-Art Stars" (page 79) and "Crow's Path," the garden tools and animals are outlined with a blanket stitch.

Below is a variety of popular embroidery stitches that can be used to add nice detail to your appliqué.

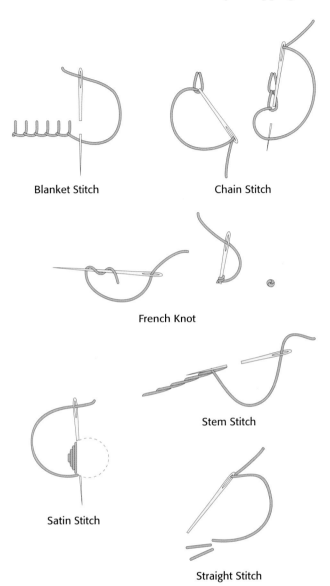

Blanket Stitch   Chain Stitch

French Knot

Stem Stitch

Satin Stitch

Straight Stitch

Remember that appliqué is only a close approximation of reality. The objects we sew will be identifiable as those they were intended to look like, but will not perfectly mimic the real model or even the pattern they came from. When I look back at the flowers I have appliquéd, I notice that no two are identical. Even though I started out with the same template, the stitching usually changes the objects so they look different from one another. Give yourself the freedom to make a new creation each time you appliqué an object, and enjoy the creative process. For me, I like to think of appliqué as pursuing the illusion of perfection, not perfection itself.

Basic Quiltmaking Techniques

When you go shopping to find just the right combination of fabrics for your two-block quilt, be sure to select fabrics that are 100% cotton. Usually the fabric will be about 42" wide, and the fabric requirements in this book are based upon that width, minus the selvages. Once you get your fabrics home, wash, dry, and press them before cutting to eliminate any chance of shrinking in the final quilt.

Before starting a new project, put a new blade in your rotary cutter. A sharp blade will make it easier to accurately cut pieces, and accurate pieces will help your blocks fit together easily. For more on rotary cutting and other basic quiltmaking techniques, read through the following sections.

ROTARY CUTTING

1. Aligning your rotary ruler with the fold of the fabric, make a clean cut from folded edge to selvage, to square up the raw edge of the fabric.

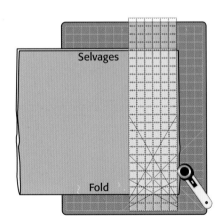

2. Turn your mat 90° and line up the ruler with your newly straightened edge to cut off about ½" of the selvage. The selvages often pull in more than the rest of the fabric, so removing them will keep your fabric from curling as you cut.

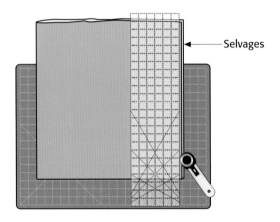

3. Turn your mat another 90° and begin cutting strips. After every three or four cuts, turn your mat back to the original position and square up the edge of the fabric again so that your strips will continue to be perpendicular to the fold.

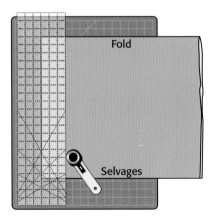

TIPS FOR MACHINE PIECING

Before sewing, check the seam-allowance guide on your sewing machine. You'll want to sew using a scant ¼" seam allowance. Accurate seams are another way to ensure that your blocks turn out perfectly. To find the "perfect ¼" seam" on your machine, cut three 1½" strips about 6" to 8" in length and sew the long edges of the strips together, pressing the seam allowances toward the outside strips.

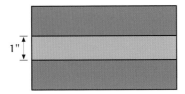

If your seams are the correct scant ¼" width, the center strip should measure exactly 1" wide. If the center strip does not measure 1", repeat the test, this time using a narrower or wider seam allowance, depending on which you need. When you find the perfect ¼" seam, layer several pieces of masking tape on the needle plate of your sewing machine to mark a guide for your fabric edges. Then, when you sew your pieces together, always guide your fabric along the masking-tape edge and your seam allowances will be consistent.

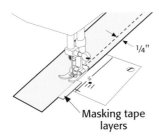

Masking tape
layers

Careful pressing after each step is important as you sew your blocks. Pressing helps ensure accurate piecing and should be done in an up-and-down fashion rather than a side-to-side motion. The objective is to get pieces to lie flat without stretching them. Many quilters make an initial press with their fingers when piecing small units, then follow up with an iron when a larger unit is pieced.

Seams are pressed to one side, as shown in the piecing diagrams in the project directions. Seams should be pressed toward the darker fabric unless other directions are given.

Now that you're ready to begin, here is more helpful information on the techniques you need to complete your quilt.

Half-Square Triangles

You can make triangle squares (two half-square triangles sewn together to make a pieced square) by cutting squares in half diagonally to make triangles and then sewing two contrasting triangles together. However, below is a shortcut method that comes in handy when you need to make a lot of triangle squares for a project.

1. Layer two same-sized squares with right sides together. Draw a diagonal pencil line from corner to corner on the wrong side of the lightest square.
2. Sew a scant ¼" from each side of the drawn line.
3. Cut on the drawn line to separate two identical triangle squares. Press the seam allowances toward the darker fabric (unless instructed otherwise in your project directions).

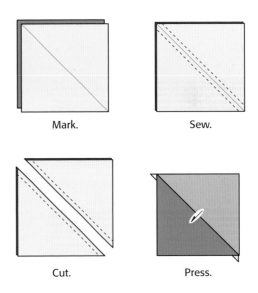

Mark.   Sew.

Cut.   Press.

Quarter-Square Triangles

I like to use this method for making quarter-square-triangle units when the triangles will always appear in the same position in the block. For instance, if the dark triangle will always be to the left of the light triangle, or vice versa, then this shortcut method for sewing the units will ensure that you don't have your triangles stitched together in the wrong position.

1. Layer two squares right sides together and draw intersecting diagonal lines from corner to corner as shown.
2. Stitch a scant ¼" from the drawn lines as shown, making sure to stop stitching where the lines intersect. Also, as you rotate the squares to stitch each subsequent seam, make sure that you're always stitching on the same side of the marked line (either always on the right or always on the

left) as shown. The instructions for each project will tell you whether to stitch on the left or right side of the lines.

3. Cut along the drawn lines and press the resulting triangles open.

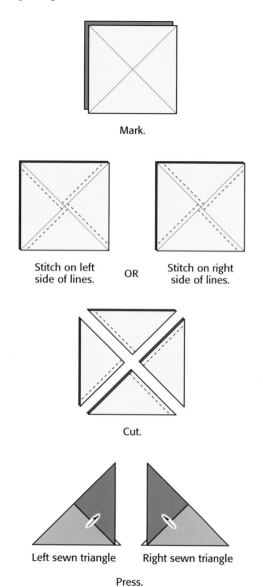

Mark.

Stitch on left
side of lines.
OR
Stitch on right
side of lines.

Cut.

Left sewn triangle   Right sewn triangle

Press.

Quick Corner Triangles

Quick corner triangles are made by sewing squares to the corners of larger squares or rectangles. After stitching diagonally along the smaller square, the excess fabric is trimmed and the result is a triangle shape.

This technique is particularly useful when dealing with very small corner triangles, which have a tendency to finish smaller than their intended size. It can also eliminate the need to cut odd-sized pieces, such as those in the border of "Crow's Path" (page 57).

The sizes of the squares or rectangles to use and how to position them are given in each project.

1. Using a pencil and ruler, draw a diagonal line on the wrong side of the square that will become the corner triangle.

2. With right sides together, pin this square on the corner of the larger piece as called for in your project directions. Sew on the drawn line.

3. Flip open the new corner triangle over the existing corner and press. If the triangle reaches the fabric edges of the underneath piece, then trim the seam to ¼" from the drawn line as shown. If the edges do not align, resew the seam and press again before trimming.

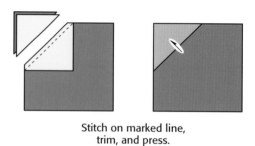

Stitch on marked line,
trim, and press.

SQUARING UP BLOCKS

Making sure that your blocks are square and a consistent size before you sew them together is important to ensure that they will fit together easily. To do this, you may want to square up the units within the blocks as you complete each stage of the piecing. For instance, after completing a flying-geese unit for a star point, turn the unit to the wrong side and measure it. Then carefully trim the edges to the correct size, being careful to leave a ¼" seam allowance from all points.

Likewise, before joining the blocks together in rows, be sure to square up or resize your blocks so that they are all the same size. Make all the blocks before you determine your average block size. For example, if the blocks should all measure 12½" but yours actually measure 12⅜", go ahead and use the 12⅜" size. If you have blocks that vary in size, you can take the average size or the most prevalent size and trim the others to this measurement.

If any of the blocks look distorted, re-pressing may help. Remember to press in an up-and-down fashion without moving the iron side to side on the fabric. If trimming is necessary, trim very carefully, allowing a ¼" seam allowance.

ADDING BORDERS

There are two different types of borders: strip borders and pieced borders. Strip borders are usually quicker and easier to make, but they can become distorted or stretched if sewn incorrectly. You will be happier with the result if you try the following methods. Likewise, you will find tips for making pieced borders and matching them to your quilt top in this section.

Strip Borders

Strip borders are made by cutting long pieces of fabric and attaching them to the edges of your finished quilt top. I like to cut strip borders on the lengthwise grain of the fabric because they are less apt to stretch. However, if you cut your border strips on the lengthwise grain, the remaining fabric will be narrower, which will require cutting more strips than indicated in cutting charts for other quilt pieces. Therefore, instructions in the patterns suggest crosswise fabric strips, which sometimes must be pieced to achieve the length of the quilt top. If strips must be pieced, join them with a 45° or 60° angle to achieve a pleasing appearance. Cutting lengthwise borders sometimes requires more fabric than cutting them crosswise. For each project where this is the case, you'll find an alternate yardage amount in case you'd like to cut your borders lengthwise.

Strip borders can be finished with squared corners or with mitered corners. Instructions for each method are given below.

Squared Corners

For this method, sew the side borders to the quilt first unless the instructions say otherwise.

1. To find the most accurate measurement for your side borders, measure the quilt through the vertical center and cut or piece the side border strips to this measurement.

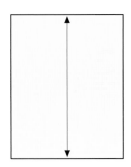

Measure vertical center.

2. Fold the quilt in half and then in fourths and mark these points with a pin. Fold and mark the border strips in the same way. Then, with right sides together, pin the strips to the sides, matching the marks. Sew the borders to the quilt top and press the seam allowances toward the side borders.

3. To determine the length of the top and bottom borders, measure the quilt horizontally across the center, including the borders you just added. Cut or piece the strips to this measurement.

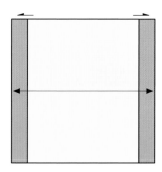

Measure horizontal center.

4. Fold, mark, and pin the border strips to the top and bottom of the quilt as you did for the side borders. Sew the borders to the quilt and press the seam allowances toward the borders.

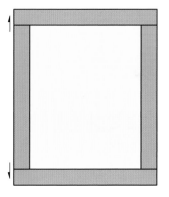

Mitered Corners

1. Just as for squared corners, measure the length of the quilt top vertically through the center. Add two times the width of your border plus 4" to your measurement; this will be the length to cut the side border strips.

2. Fold the quilt top in half and then in fourths and place pins at these points.

3. Mark the length of the quilt onto the border strip using straight pins. Then, fold the border strip in half, aligning the two end pins, to find the

midpoint of the border. Mark the midpoint, and then fold in half again to mark the border in fourths. With right sides together, pin the border strips to the sides of the quilt top, matching the pins.

4. With right sides together, sew the borders to the sides of the quilt top, stopping and backstitching ¼" from the pin at each end.

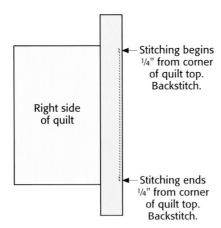

Right side of quilt

Stitching begins ¼" from corner of quilt top. Backstitch.

Stitching ends ¼" from corner of quilt top. Backstitch.

5. For the top and bottom borders, measure the quilt horizontally through the center. Add two times the width of your border plus 4" to this measurement; this will be the length to cut or piece the top and bottom border strips. Measure and mark the end points as well as the midpoint and quarter points on the border and quilt top. Pin the borders in place and stitch as before, starting and stopping ¼" from each end of the quilt top. Note that the border strips will extend beyond each end of the quilt and overlap the side borders. Press the seam allowances toward the borders.

6. To create the miters, work with the quilt right side up and lay one strip on top of the adjacent border. Fold the top border under at a 45° angle so that it aligns with the adjacent border. Press and pin the fold in place.

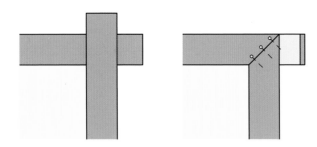

7. Position a 90° triangle or Bias Square ruler over the corner to check that the corner is flat and square. Unpin the crease, adjust, if necessary, and re-press the fold firmly to create a crease.

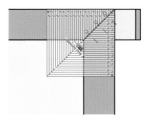

8. Fold the center section of the quilt top diagonally from the corner so the right sides are together, aligning the long edges of the borders. On the wrong side, draw a pencil line along the diagonal crease of the border and position the pins on both sides of the drawn line.

9. Beginning at the inside corner, backstitch and then stitch along the crease toward the outside point, being careful not to stitch into the quilt top or to stretch the fabric. Backstitch at the end of the seam. Turn the quilt top over and check the mitered corner. If the corner is acceptable, turn the quilt to the back side and trim the excess border fabric to ¼". Press the seam allowances to one side. Repeat to complete all four corners.

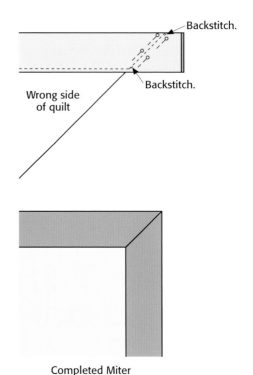

Backstitch.

Wrong side of quilt

Backstitch.

Completed Miter

Pieced Borders

Sewing a pieced border onto a pieced quilt can be tricky. Making sure that the seams line up usually requires pinning. The following tips can make matching points easier and take less time than resewing.

Matching same-sized patches. If the patches of the border are the same size as the patches of the quilt, all or most of the seams will line up. Pin on either side of each seam, laying seams in opposing directions. Pinning will help ensure that the seams stay lined up and don't shift as you sew the border in place. Occasionally you may have to re-press seams so they lie in opposing directions. By following pressing arrows in the step-by-step assembly diagrams, you should be able to avoid this situation.

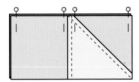

Aligning different-sized patches. If the patches of the border are larger or smaller than those in the quilt top, you may have to use one of several techniques to ensure a well fitted border.

1. Fold the border, matching seams that are on either side of the large patch, such as in "Folk-Art Stars" on page 79 where a trapezoid is used in the border. Place a pin on the fold of the trapezoid, marking its center. When matching the border to the quilt, pin the border where the seams will align automatically first. Then line up the pins with the alternate seams on the quilt top.

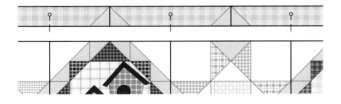

2. Sometimes the border seams will not match up due to a disproportionate number of seams between the blocks and the border. If there are more seams in the quilt blocks than in the pieced border, the blocks may "shrink" to less than their intended size. When that happens, you must take bigger seams when piecing the border. Usually, using an exact ¼" seam instead of a scant ¼" when you are piecing the border will alleviate this problem.

3. If your pieced border consists of large rectangular pieces, such as in "Feathered Flowers" on page 71, the pieces may need to be trimmed to match the block size. Measure the size of the pieced block (including outer seam allowances) and trim the large rectangles to that size.

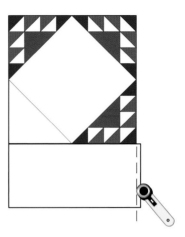

Finishing the Quilt

To finish the quilt, you will need to make the quilt sandwich, which consists of your quilt top, the batting, and the quilt backing. After securing the layers with pin or thread basting, you will need to hand or machine quilt the layers together. The edges will be finished with binding. Depending upon the function of your quilt, you may want to add a sleeve for hanging. This section will guide you through all of these finishing steps.

Layering and Basting

If your quilt is to be quilted on a long-arm quilting machine, it is helpful to sew a 2"–3" strip of fabric to each edge of the quilt top. The added strip provides a pinning strip for the quilter, where she can attach your quilt top to the canvas leader on her frame. With the pinning strip attached, the quilter will be able to quilt right up to your quilt edge and you won't have to worry about any seams in a pieced border being stretched apart when the quilt is pulled taut onto the frame.

Before layering your quilt top, batting, and backing, press the entire top. Be sure to snip any long or raveling threads from the back to prevent them from showing through the quilt top. With the wrong side of the backing up, layer the batting on top of the backing. Place the quilt top, right side up, on the batting. Smooth out all layers, creating a flat, even, wrinkle-free surface. (You can eliminate wrinkles in your batting by tumbling it in the dryer for 5 to 10 minutes on air only, no heat.)

If you choose to hand quilt, baste the layers together with cotton basting thread in horizontal and vertical rows approximately 6" to 8" apart.

If you prefer to machine quilt, use safety pins spaced 4"–6" apart for holding the layers together. The pins will be easy to remove as your stitching nears them, while thread basting can be tricky to remove after it has been stitched over repeatedly by machine.

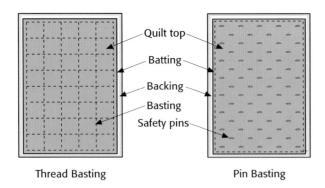

Thread Basting   Pin Basting

Machine Quilting

For best results, use a walking foot and a needle designed for machine quilting. Loosen the top tension of your machine by half of one number setting to prevent the bottom thread from being pulled up to the top. The top thread can be cotton, cotton-wrapped polyester, or nylon monofilament. I match the thread color and weight of the top and bobbin to achieve uniform stitches and to prevent the bottom color from showing on the quilt top. To avoid tying threads and to secure quilting lines, begin and end with several very small stitches, and then clip the thread tails close to the quilt surface.

Hand Quilting

For hand quilting I recommend a Between needle, size 9–12, and cotton quilting thread. Secure the quilt in a freestanding or lap hoop and draw it taut. Thread the needle and make a small knot at the end of the thread, trimming the tail to about ⅛". Push the needle through the quilt top and batting ¾" to 1" away from the place you intend to start quilting. Gently pull the knot under the fabric, securing it in the batting, and come back up where you want to start quilting. If the knot continues to come back up through the top, make a bigger knot or try to start your quilting at a seam, securing the knot in the seam

allowance. Push the needle straight down with a thimble. Come up a short distance away and make a rocking motion with the needle to create several short running stitches.

You can end stitching in two ways. For the first method, wrap the thread around the needle two or three times, push the needle through the quilt top and batting layers only, and bring the tip back up about a needle's length away. Pull the thread through the layers and gently pop the resulting knot through the fabric. After you hear the knot pop, gently pull the thread a little further, push back the quilt top slightly, and snip the thread. When the quilt is smoothed out again, the cut end of the tail will be hidden in the layers.

The second method is for quilters who want to avoid knots. Rotate your quilt, if possible, and take four or five backstitches over the previously made stitches. Then push the needle under the quilt top and bring it back up a needle's distance away. Snip the thread as described above.

Adding a Hanging Sleeve

If you plan to hang your quilt, sew a hanging sleeve to the top back of the quilt at the time the binding is added. Cut an 8½"-wide strip of fabric that is 1" shorter in length than the width of the quilt top. Turn under the short ends of the strip ½" and machine stitch them in place. Then, with wrong sides together, fold the strip lengthwise and press.

After squaring up your completed quilt with a rotary cutter and long ruler to remove the excess batting and backing, center the sleeve at the top edge of the quilt back, matching the unfinished edges, and pin. Using a fat ⅛" seam allowance, machine baste in place. You may want to pin the folded edge to the quilt back to keep it from getting caught in the seam when sewing on the binding. After completing the binding, hand stitch the bottom fold of the sleeve to the quilt back, using a blind stitch.

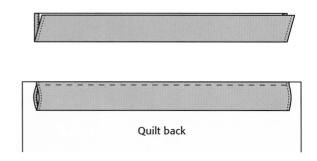

Quilt back

Binding

1. Sew the binding strips together end to end with 45° or 60° diagonal seams to make one continuous strip. Cut the beginning end of the strip at the same angle. Press under the beginning end of the strip ¼". Fold the pieced strip lengthwise, wrong sides together, and press.

    Note: Cutting the ends of strips at an angle will prevent lumps in the binding.

2. Matching raw edges, place the beginning of the binding about halfway down one side of the front of the quilt. Begin stitching about 3" away from the end of the binding, taking a few backstitches and using a scant ¼" seam allowance. Leave the beginning 3" unstitched for now.

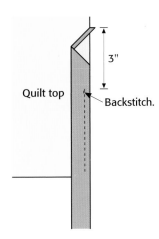

3. Stop ¼" away from the corner of the quilt and, with the needle still in the fabric, pivot the quilt 45° and stitch to the outer corner of the quilt and backstitch.

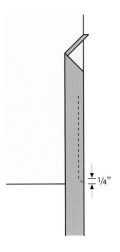

4. Lift the needle and remove the quilt from the machine. Fold the binding strip up away from the quilt so that it is perpendicular to the part you've just attached. Then fold it back down, even with the edge of the quilt. The folded edge should be flush with the adjacent edge of the quilt. Begin sewing at the folded edge and sew to ¼" from the next corner.

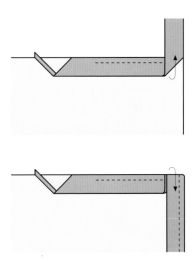

5. Repeat steps 3 and 4 at each corner. Stop sewing 3" from where you started attaching the binding, backstitch, and remove the quilt from the machine. Trim the binding end at an angle, leaving enough fabric to tuck into the folded beginning tail.

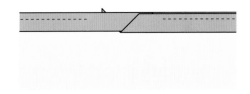

6. After tucking the ending tail into the beginning tail, pin and finish sewing the binding to the quilt. Turn the folded edge to the back side of the quilt and hand stitch it in place. If you have added a hanging sleeve to your quilt, hand sew the folded bottom edge to the quilt back, using a blind stitch.

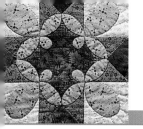

Aunt Bee

Designed by Claudia Olson; made and hand quilted by Doni Palmgren, 2001, Wenatchee, Washington.

"Aunt Bee" uses an Aunt Sukey block variation along with an Ohio Star variation that I call Honeybee Star. Large open spaces between the corners of the two blocks make an ideal place for the bees to land and for the quilter to quilt. Notice how the gold bees are set on top of the star blocks, where they appear to be gathered around a red square doing a honey dance. In the Aunt Sukey blocks, an on-point square is created by the red and dark green triangles that frame the blocks, so allow these fabrics to dominate and they'll make a statement in your quilt.

Finished Quilt Size: 45½" x 45½"
Finished Block Size: 9"

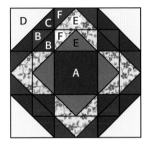
Aunt Sukey Block

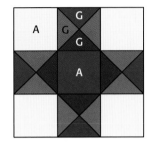
Honeybee Star Block

MATERIALS

Yardages are based on 42"-wide fabrics.

1½ yards of medium green print for Honeybee Star blocks, borders, and binding*

⅞ yard of red-and-gold floral for Aunt Sukey blocks and border

¾ yard of dark green print for blocks and pieced border

⅝ yard of beige print for background

½ yard of red print for blocks

⅜ yard of gold print for bee appliqués

¼ yard of light green print for Aunt Sukey blocks

2 yards of backing fabric

51" x 51" piece of batting

Optional: ¼ yard of lightweight interfacing for appliqués

The yardage given is enough for borders cut across the width of the fabric. If you prefer to cut lengthwise borders, you'll need 1⅜ yards of red-and-gold floral.

AUNTIE'S ANGELS

Designed by Claudia Olson; made by Pat Peyton, 2002, Pocatello, Idaho; quilted by Jill Therriault. Notice how this quilt uses the same blocks but varies the color placement. In addition, Pat uses angels rather than bee appliqués for this Christmas variation.

Cutting for 4 Aunt Sukey Blocks

Fabric	Piece	Number of Strips	Strip Width	First Cut	Second Cut
Red	B	1	2⅜"	8 squares, 2⅜" x 2⅜"	
	F	2	2"	32 squares, 2" x 2"	
Dark green	A	1	3½"	4 squares, 3½" x 3½"	
	B	1	2⅜"	8 squares, 2⅜" x 2⅜"	
	C	1	2⅜"	16 squares, 2⅜" x 2⅜"	Cut ◻ to yield 32 triangles
Beige	D	1	3⅞"	8 squares, 3⅞" x 3⅞"	Cut ◻ to yield 16 triangles
Floral	E	1	3½"	16 rectangles, 2" x 3½"	
	F	2	2"	32 squares, 2" x 2"	
Light green	E	1	3½"	16 rectangles, 2" x 3½"	

PIECING THE AUNT SUKEY BLOCKS

1. Referring to "Half-Square Triangles" on page 23, position a red B square on a dark green B square. Stitch, cut, and press. Make eight to yield 16 triangle squares.

2. Sew two dark green C triangles to the red sides of the triangle squares from step 1 as shown. Then sew a beige D triangle to these pieced triangles as shown. Make 16.

3. Referring to "Quick Corner Triangles" on page 24, position a red F square on the end of a floral E rectangle. Stitch, cut, and press. Repeat, stitching a red corner on the other end of the rectangle. Make 16. Repeat the process, stitching floral F squares on the corners of light green E rectangles. Make 16. Sew the completed flying-geese units together in pairs as shown, with the green triangle on the bottom. Press the seam allowances toward the top unit.

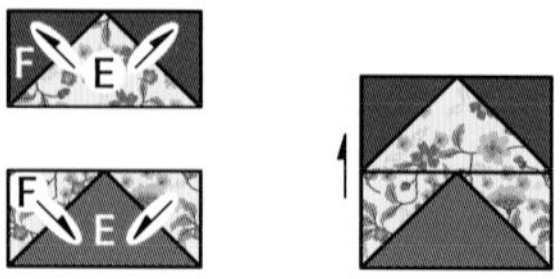

4. Lay out the pieced units from steps 2 and 3, along with a dark green A square, as shown. Sew the units together in rows.

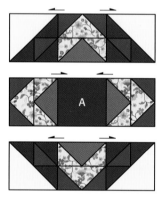

5. Sew the rows together to complete one Aunt Sukey block. Repeat to make four blocks.

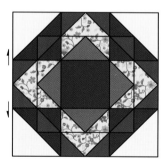

Aunt Sukey Block
Make 4.

Cutting for 5 Honeybee Star Blocks				
Fabric	**Piece**	**Number of Strips**	**Strip Width**	**First Cut**
Medium green	G	2	4¼"	10 squares, 4¼" x 4¼"
Red	G	1	4¼"	5 squares, 4¼" x 4¼"
	A	1	3½"	5 squares, 3½" x 3½"
Dark green	G	1	4¼"	5 squares, 4¼" x 4¼"
Beige	A	2	3½"	20 squares, 3½" x 3½"

MAKING THE HONEYBEE STAR BLOCKS

1. Referring to "Quarter-Square Triangles" on page 23, position a medium green G square on top of a red G square, right sides together. Stitch to the right side of your drawn lines, cut the units apart, and press the seam allowances toward the green triangles. Stitch five to yield 20 quarter-square triangles.

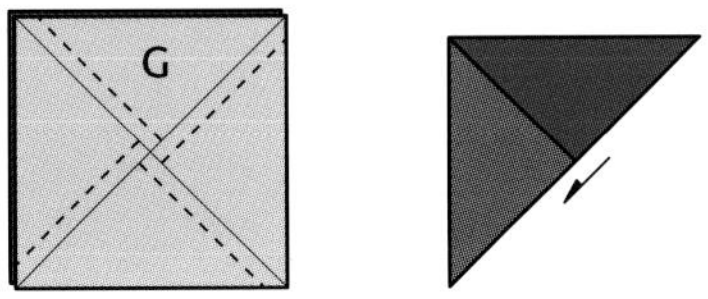

2. Repeat step 1, using a medium green G square on top of a dark green G square. Stitch to the right side of the drawn lines, cut the units apart, and press the seam allowances toward the medium green triangles. Stitch five to yield 20 quarter-square triangles.

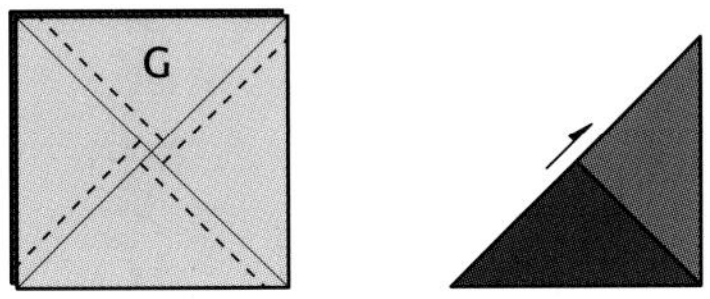

3. Sew the triangle units from step 1 to those made in step 2 as shown. Make 20.

4. Lay out four pieced squares with one red A square and four beige A squares as shown. Sew the pieced and plain squares together in rows.

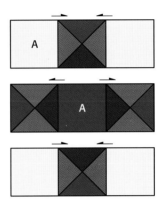

5. Sew the rows together to complete a Honeybee Star block. Repeat to make five blocks.

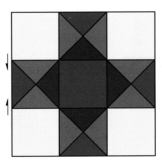

Honeybee Star Block
Make 5.

6. Referring to "Appliqué Techniques" on page 12, use the method of your choice to prepare 20 honeybee appliqués (patterns on page 35). If your bees are light gold, back them with interfacing to prevent the dark green from showing through. Position the bee pieces on the blocks referring to the quilt photograph on page 30 or the quilt assembly diagram on page 34 for placement. Stitch in place.

Cutting for Borders and Binding				
Fabric	Piece	Number of Strips	Strip Width	First Cut
Beige	D	3	3⅞"	14 squares, 3⅞" x 3⅞"
Dark green	D	3	3⅞"	14 squares, 3⅞" x 3⅞"
Medium green	E	1	3½"	12 rectangles, 2" x 3½"
	F	2	2"	24 squares, 2" x 2"
	Borders 2 and 4	9	2"	
	Binding	5	2¼"	
Red	E	1	3½"	12 rectangles, 2" x 3½"
Floral	Border 3	5	3½"	

MAKING THE PIECED BORDER

1. Referring to "Half-Square Triangles" on page 23, position a beige D square on a dark green D square. Stitch, cut, and press. Make 14 of these squares to yield 28 triangle squares.

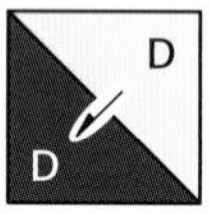

2. Referring to "Quick Corner Triangles" on page 24, position a medium green F square on the end of a red E rectangle. Stitch, cut, and press. Repeat to make a medium green corner on the other end. Make 12 units. Sew a medium green E rectangle to the top edge of each pieced rectangle as shown.

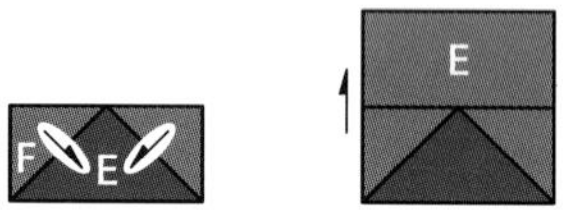

3. Sew the triangle squares from step 1 to opposite sides of the unit made in step 2 as shown. Make 12.

4. Sew three units from step 3 together as shown to make a complete border. Repeat to make a total of four pieced borders. Sew a triangle square from step 1 to opposite ends of two of the borders as shown.

Make 2.

Make 2.

ASSEMBLING THE QUILT TOP

1. Lay out the quilt blocks in three rows of three blocks each, alternating the Honeybee Star and Aunt Sukey blocks as shown. Sew the blocks together in rows and then join the rows. Press.
2. Sew the shorter pieced borders to opposite sides of the quilt top. Press the seam allowances toward the borders. Then sew the longer pieced borders to the top and bottom of the quilt top. Press as before.

Quilt Assembly

3. Sew the 2"-wide medium green strips together end to end. From this long strip, cut four segments 41" long for the second border. Cut four segments that are 48" long for the fourth border. In the same manner, piece together the 3½"-wide floral strips and cut four segments 44" long for the third border.

4. Measure the border strips and mark the midpoints with a pin. Pin and then sew together a 2" x 41" medium green strip, a 3½" x 44" floral strip, and a 2" x 48" medium green strip, matching the midpoints. Repeat to make four border units.

5. Referring to "Mitered Corners" on page 25, attach a border unit to each side of the quilt and miter the corners. Press.

FINISHING THE QUILT

Referring to "Finishing the Quilt" on page 27, prepare the backing fabric and then layer the backing, batting, and quilt top. After basting the layers together, hand or machine quilt as desired and then bind your quilt, using the 2¼"-wide medium green strips.

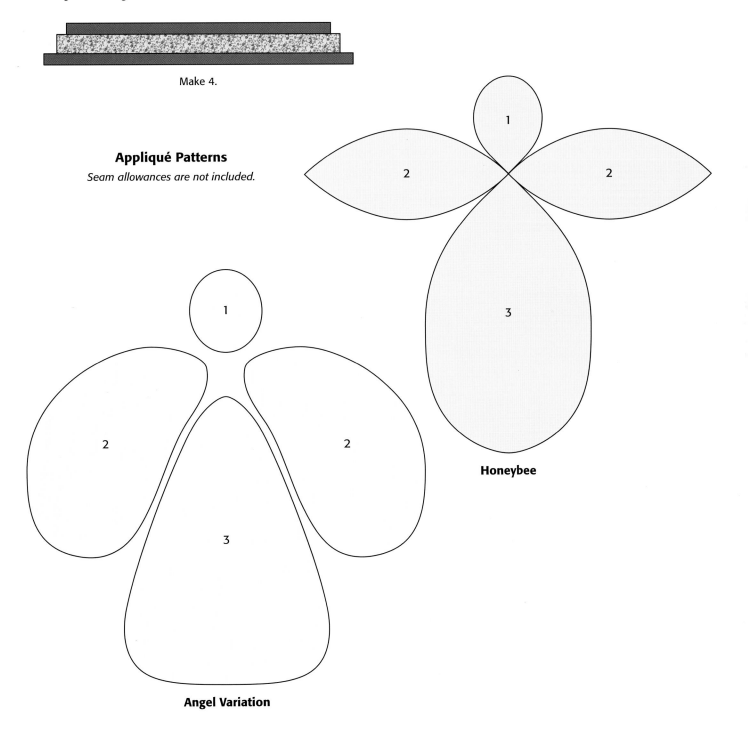

Make 4.

Appliqué Patterns
Seam allowances are not included.

1

2

2

3

Honeybee

1

2

2

3

Angel Variation

Windblown Pinwheels

Designed by Claudia Olson; made and machine quilted by Karen Sinn, 2002, Wenatchee, Washington.

Karen Sinn appliquéd cheerful flowers in Windblown Square Variation blocks and combined them with Broken Pinwheel blocks to create "Windblown Pinwheels." By using cool, light green prints for the background and bright, warm prints for the pinwheels, the quilter can draw the viewer's attention to the pinwheels. Use darker prints in the triangles that surround the center square in the Windblown Square Variation blocks to form a secondary star pattern.

Finished Quilt Size: 48" x 48"
Finished Block Size: 8"

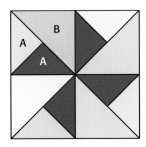

Broken Pinwheel Block

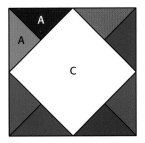

Windblown Square
Variation Block

MATERIALS

Yardages are based on 42"-wide fabrics.

1½ yards of blue-violet print for Windblown Square Variation blocks, outer border, and binding*

1 yard total of assorted light green prints for Broken Pinwheel blocks and appliqués

⅝ yard total of assorted yellow prints for Broken Pinwheel blocks, appliqués, and inner border*

½ yard of white print for Windblown Square Variation blocks

½ yard total of assorted medium green prints for Broken Pinwheel blocks and appliqués

⅜ yard of red print for Broken Pinwheel blocks and appliqués

⅜ yard total of assorted hot pink prints for Broken Pinwheel blocks and appliqués

⅜ yard total of assorted red-violet prints for Broken Pinwheel blocks and appliqués

⅜ yard total of assorted purple prints for Windblown Square Variation blocks

¼ yard of red-orange print for appliqués

¼ yard of orange print for Broken Pinwheel blocks and appliqués

¼ yard of dark blue print (or assorted scraps) for Windblown Square Variation blocks

¼ yard of turquoise print for Windblown Square Variation blocks

¼ yard of teal print for Windblown Square Variation blocks

¼ yard of dark green print (or assorted scraps) for Windblown Square Variation blocks

⅛ yard of pink print for appliqués

⅛ yard of light orange print for appliqués

3 yards of backing fabric

54" x 54" piece of batting

*The yardage given is enough for borders cut across the width of the fabric. If you prefer to cut lengthwise borders, you'll need 1⅝ yards of blue-violet print and 1⅓ yards of yellow print.

Cutting for 13 Broken Pinwheel Blocks

Fabric	Piece	Number of Strips	Strip Width	First Cut	Second Cut
Light greens	A	2	5¼"	13 squares, 5¼" x 5¼"	
	B	4	4⅞"	26 squares, 4⅞" x 4⅞"	Cut all squares ◺
Red	A	1	5¼"	2 squares, 5¼" x 5¼"	
Hot pinks	A	1	5¼"	2 squares, 5¼" x 5¼"	
Red-violets	A	1	5¼"	3 squares, 5¼" x 5¼"	
Orange	A	1	5¼"	2 squares, 5¼" x 5¼"	
Yellows	A	1	5¼"	4 squares, 5¼" x 5¼"	

PIECING THE BROKEN PINWHEEL BLOCKS

1. Referring to "Quarter-Square Triangles" on page 23, position a light green A square on a red A square. Sew to the left side of the drawn lines, cut, and press. Repeat, using each red, hot pink, red-violet, orange, and yellow A square paired with a light green A square. Each pair of squares will yield enough triangles for one pinwheel unit.

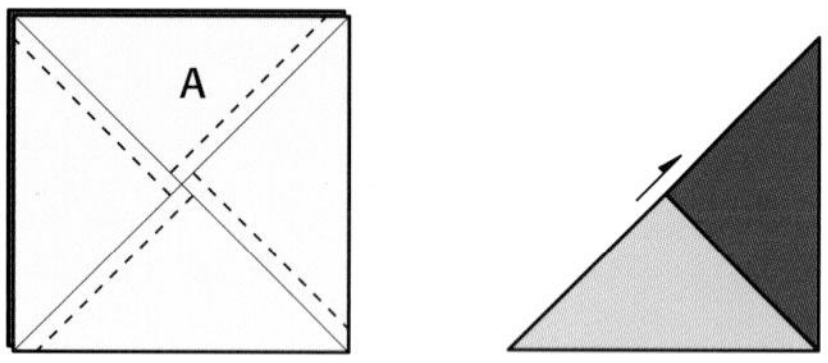

2. Sew a light green B triangle to each pair of triangles from step 1 as shown.

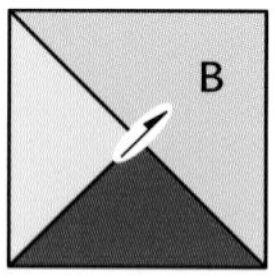

3. Sew four pieced squares from step 2 with matching red triangles together to form a Broken Pinwheel block. The light green background triangles can be of assorted fabrics, but the main color of each pinwheel should match. Make 13 blocks: two red, two hot pink, four yellow, two orange, and three red-violet.

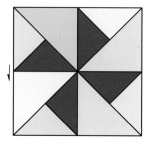

Broken Pinwheel Block
Make 13.

Cutting for 12 Windblown Square Variation Blocks

Note: *To cut the 6³⁄₁₆" squares, measure midway between the 6⅛" and 6¼" markings on your ruler.*

Fabric	Piece	Number of Strips	Strip Width	First Cut
Teal	A	1	5¼"	4 squares, 5¼" x 5¼"
Purples	A	1	5¼"	4 squares, 5¼" x 5¼"
Turquoise	A	1	5¼"	2 squares, 5¼" x 5¼"
Dark blue	A	1	5¼"	6 squares, 5¼" x 5¼"
Dark green	A	1	5¼"	4 squares, 5¼" x 5¼"
Blue-violet	A	1	5¼"	4 squares, 5¼" x 5¼"
White	C	2	6³⁄₁₆"	12 squares, 6³⁄₁₆" x 6³⁄₁₆"

PIECING THE WINDBLOWN SQUARE BLOCKS

1. Referring to "Quarter-Square Triangles" on page 23, position a teal A square on a purple A square. Sew on the left side of the drawn lines as you did in step 1 of "Piecing the Broken Pinwheel Blocks," opposite. Cut and press the units. Repeat, using various color combinations, such as turquoise with dark blue, dark green with purple, or dark blue with purple. Make 12 sets to yield 48 pairs of triangles.

2. Sew a triangle pair from step 1 to opposite sides of a white C square as shown.

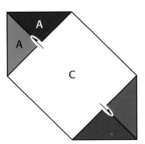

Make 12.

3. Sew a triangle pair to the remaining sides of the white square to complete the Windblown Square Variation block. Repeat for all 12 blocks, making

sure to mix up the color triangles for nice variation in your blocks.

Windblown Square Variation Block
Make 12.

ADDING THE APPLIQUÉ

1. Referring to "Appliqué Techniques" on page 12, use the method of your choice to prepare the flower petals, flower centers, and leaves (patterns on page 41). Refer to the quilt photograph on page 36 for color-placement ideas.

2. Using medium green fabric, cut bias strips 1⅛" wide. Prepare the bias stems, referring to "Stems and Branches" on page 18. From the long bias strips, cut 12 stems, each at least 2" long.

3. Referring to the appliqué placement guide on page 41, turn under the bottom end of a stem and appliqué it in place on the white center square of a Windblown Square Variation block. Choose two sets of four flower petals with coordinating colors. Appliqué the first set of petals (2–5) to the white background. Appliqué the other set of petals (6–9) to the background, overlapping the first set of petals. Appliqué a flower center over the petal centers. Finally, appliqué the leaves, noting that they do not touch the stems.

Cutting for Borders and Binding			
Fabric	**Piece**	**Number of Strips**	**Strip Width**
Yellows	Inner border	5	1½"
Blue-violet	Outer border	6	3½"
	Binding	5	2¼"

ASSEMBLING THE QUILT TOP

1. Lay out the Broken Pinwheel and Windblown Square Variation blocks in five rows of five blocks each, beginning with a Broken Pinwheel block and alternating the blocks as shown in the quilt assembly diagram below. Rearrange the blocks until you are satisfied with the color placement of the pinwheels and flowers.

2. Sew the blocks together in rows and then join the rows.

3. Sew the 1½"-wide yellow border strips together end to end. From this long strip cut four border strips, each 46" long. In the same manner, sew the 3½"-wide blue-violet border strips together end to end, and from the long strip cut four border strips, each 52" long. Matching midpoints, pin and sew each yellow strip to a blue-violet strip.

4. Referring to "Mitered Corners" on page 25, attach the borders, placing the narrow yellow strips toward the quilt center. Miter the corners to complete the quilt top.

FINISHING THE QUILT

Referring to "Finishing the Quilt" on page 27, prepare the backing fabric and then layer the backing, batting, and quilt top. After basting the layers together, hand or machine quilt as desired and then bind your quilt, using the 2¼"-wide blue-violet strips.

Quilt Assembly

Appliqué Patterns

Seam allowances are not included.

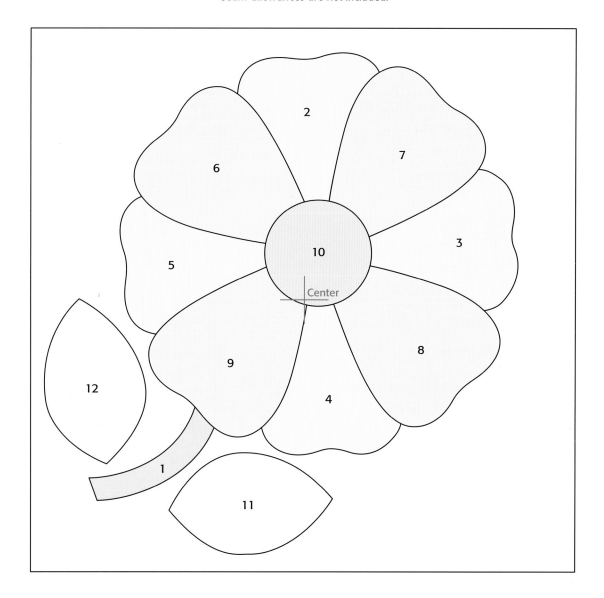

Azalea Album

Designed by Claudia Olson; made and hand quilted by Sandy Ashbrook, 2001, East Wenatchee, Washington.

"Azalea Album" combines Lighthouse Beacon blocks and Album blocks. By substituting some of the dark-colored block corners with a white print, we create an area for appliqué after the blocks are joined. With careful fabric selection, a medallion-type center also appears, adding emphasis to the bright pink azalea flowers that are appliquéd on the white squares. Notice how the blooms are surrounded by stars of purple, green, and yellow.

Finished Quilt Size: 48" x 48"
Finished Block Size: 12"

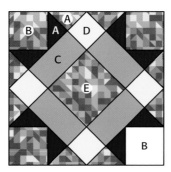

Lighthouse Beacon Block

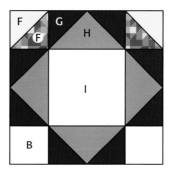

Album Block

MATERIALS

Yardages are based on 42"-wide fabrics.

2⅛ yards of floral print for blocks, borders, and binding*

1 yard of purple print for blocks and pieced border

⅝ yard of medium green print for Lighthouse Beacon blocks and pieced border

½ yard of lavender print for Album blocks and pieced border

½ yard of yellow print for blocks and pieced border

½ yard of white print for blocks

⅜ yard of dark green print for appliqués

⅜ yard total of assorted bright pink prints for appliqués

2½ yards of backing fabric

54" x 54" piece of batting

Gold metallic thread

The yardage given is enough for borders to be cut lengthwise or crosswise.

Cutting for 5 Lighthouse Beacon Blocks				
Fabric	**Piece**	**Number of Strips**	**Strip Width**	**First Cut**
Floral	A	2	4¼"	10 squares, 4¼" x 4¼"
	B	2	3½"	15 squares, 3½" x 3½"
	E	1	4¾"	5 squares, 4¾" x 4¾"
Purple	A	2	4¼"	10 squares, 4¼" x 4¼"
White	B	1	3½"	8 squares, 3½" x 3½"
Medium green	C	2	4¾"	20 rectangles, 2⅝" x 4¾"
Yellow	D	2	2⅝"	20 squares, 2⅝" x 2⅝"

PIECING THE LIGHTHOUSE BEACON BLOCKS

Referring to the piecing instructions and diagrams below, make five Lighthouse Beacon blocks. Note that four of the blocks have one white corner, while the fifth block has four white corners.

1. Referring to "Half-Square Triangles" on page 23, position a floral A square on a purple A square. Stitch, cut, and press. Make 10 to yield 20 triangle squares. Then cut the squares in half diagonally, in the opposite direction of the seam line. You'll have 40 triangle pairs.

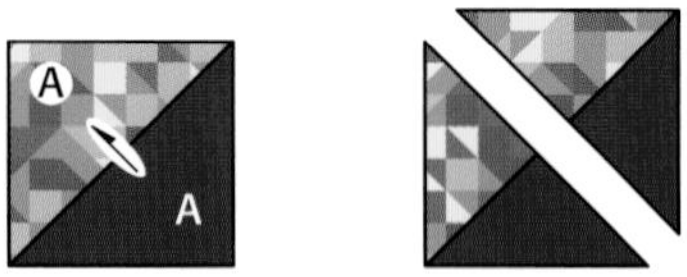

2. Sew the triangle pairs to two adjacent sides of 12 floral B squares as shown. Repeat, sewing triangle pairs to two adjacent sides of eight white B squares.

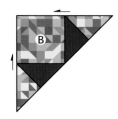 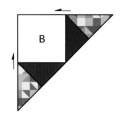

3. Lay out the medium green C rectangles, yellow D squares, and floral E squares as shown. Sew the pieces together in rows and then join the rows. Repeat to make five units.

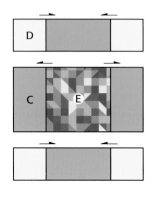 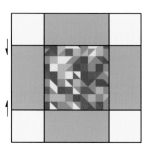

Make 5.

4. Sew the large pieced triangles with the **floral** B squares made in step 2 to opposite sides of four of the units from step 3.

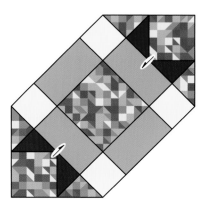

5. Sew another matching pieced triangle to one of the remaining sides. To the final side, attach a pieced triangle with a **white** B square.

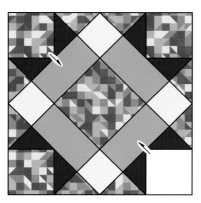

Lighthouse Beacon Block
Make 4.

6. In the same manner, make one more block, this time sewing the remaining pieced triangles with **white** B squares to each side of the center unit.

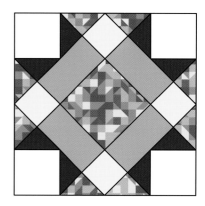

Lighthouse Beacon Block
Make 1.

Cutting for 4 Album Blocks				
Fabric	**Piece**	**Number of Strips**	**Strip Width**	**First Cut**
Yellow	F	1	3⅞"	4 squares, 3⅞" x 3⅞"
Floral	F	1	3⅞"	4 squares, 3⅞" x 3⅞"
Purple	B	3	3½"	32 squares, 3½" x 3½"
Lavender	H	2	6½"	16 rectangles, 3½" x 6½"
White	B	1	3½"	8 squares, 3½" x 3½"
	I	1	6½"	4 squares, 6½" x 6½"

PIECING THE ALBUM BLOCKS

1. Referring to "Half-Square Triangles" on page 23, position a yellow F square on a floral F square. Stitch, cut, and press. Make four to yield eight triangle squares.

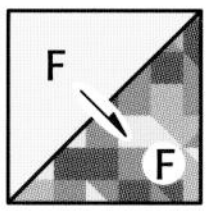

2. Referring to "Quick Corner Triangles" on page 24, position a purple B square on the end of a lavender H rectangle. Stitch, cut, and press. Repeat, adding a purple corner on the other end of the rectangle. Make 16 of these flying-geese units.

3. Sew a triangle square from step 1 on each end of four of the flying-geese units from step 2 as shown. Sew a white B square on each end of four flying-geese units.

Make 4.

Make 4.

4. Sew the eight remaining flying-geese units to opposite sides of the four white I squares.

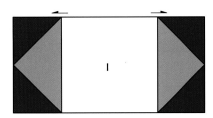

5. Lay out the two different flying-geese units from step 3 and the unit from step 4 in rows. Sew the rows together to complete four Album blocks as shown.

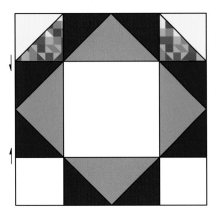

Album Block
Make 4.

ADDING THE APPLIQUÉ

Referring to "Appliqué Techniques" on page 12, use the method of your choice to prepare the appliqué shapes for the azalea flowers (patterns on pages 48 and 49). You can appliqué four of the designs now in the center of the Album blocks. After assembling the quilt top, appliqué the flowers in the newly created white squares. In the quilt shown, the following blocks were used:

Block 1: Make 2 and 1 reversed

Block 2: Make 1

Block 3: Make 1 and 1 reversed

Block 4: Make 1 and 1 reversed

Some of the blocks can be completely appliquéd now. Others overlap the boundaries into the adjacent blocks and will need to be completed after the quilt top has been assembled.

Referring to the appliqué patterns, sew the stems and leaves to the background fabric first. Then appliqué the flower petals in the sequence indicated. Last, add embroidery detail in the flower centers. Use gold metallic thread to embroider the stamens using a stem stitch and French knots. (See page 21 for stitch illustrations.)

Cutting for Borders and Binding				
Fabric	**Piece**	**Number of Strips**	**Strip Width**	**First Cut**
Yellow	F	1	3⅞"	8 squares, 3⅞" x 3⅞"
Medium green	F	2	3⅞"	12 squares, 3⅞" x 3⅞"
Lavender	H	1	6½"	8 rectangles, 3½" x 6½"
Purple	G	3	3½"	24 squares, 3½" x 3½"
Floral	F	1	3⅞"	4 squares, 3⅞" x 3⅞"
	B	1	3½"	4 squares, 3½" x 3½"
	H	Use remainder of 3½" strip above	3½"	4 rectangles, 3½" x 6½"
	Border	6	3½"	
	Binding	6	2¼"	

Making the Pieced Border

1. Referring to "Half-Square Triangles" on page 23, position a yellow F square on a medium green F square. Stitch, cut, and press. Make eight to yield 16 triangle squares. Repeat, making four to yield 8 medium green/floral triangle squares in the same manner.

Make 16.　　　Make 8.

2. Follow step 2 from "Piecing the Album Blocks" to make eight lavender/purple flying-geese units, using the lavender H rectangles and purple G squares. In the same manner, repeat, making four floral/purple flying-geese units.

Make 8.　　　Make 4.

3. Sew a yellow/green triangle square to each side of a lavender/purple flying-geese unit as shown. Make eight. Sew a green/floral triangle square to each side of a floral/purple flying-geese unit as shown. Make four.

Make 8.

Make 4.

4. Sew the purple/lavender flying-geese units to each end of the purple/floral flying-geese units to make four pieced borders. Sew a floral B square to each end of two of the pieced borders.

Make 2.

Make 2.

Assembling the Quilt Top

1. Lay out the quilt blocks in three rows of three blocks each, alternating Lighthouse Beacon and Album blocks as shown. Sew the blocks together in rows and then join the rows. Press. At this point you can finish your appliqué.

2. Referring to the quilt assembly diagram below for orientation, sew the two shorter pieced borders to the sides of the quilt top, matching the seams. Press the seam allowances toward the borders. In the same manner, attach the longer pieced borders to the top and bottom of the quilt.

3. Sew the 3½"-wide floral strips together end to end to make four border strips at least 52" long. Referring to "Mitered Corners" on page 25, attach one border strip to each side of the quilt and miter the corners.

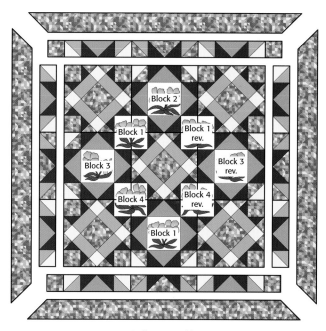

Quilt Assembly

Finishing the Quilt

Referring to "Finishing the Quilt" on page 27, prepare the backing fabric and then layer the backing, batting, and quilt top. After basting the layers together, hand or machine quilt as desired and then bind your quilt, using the 2¼"-wide floral strips.

Appliqué Patterns

Enlarge patterns 133%.

Seam allowances are not included.

Embroider details as indicated.

········· Stem stitch

⋮ French knot

Block 1
Make 2 and 1 reversed.

Block 2
Make 1.

Appliqué Patterns

Enlarge patterns 133%.

Seam allowances are not included.

Embroider details as indicated.

-------- Stem stitch

⊙ French knot

Block 3
Make 1 and 1 reversed.

Block 4
Make 1 and 1 reversed.

Crossed Stars

Designed by Claudia Olson; made by LaVanche Rhodes, 2001, Wenatchee, Washington;
machine quilted by Jill Therriault.

"Crossed Stars" is made with a Sawtooth Star Variation block and a Double Cross block. The Double Cross block provides a perfect space for appliqué. Holly leaves and berries give the quilt a Christmas sparkle, and for an extra bit of fun, quiltmaker LaVanche Rhodes used maroon buttons for her berries. Using red triangles as corners in the Double Cross blocks makes a secondary star appear around the Sawtooth Stars when the blocks are joined.

Finished Quilt Size: 52" x 76"
Finished Block Size: 12"

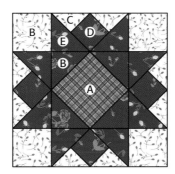

Sawtooth Star Variation Block

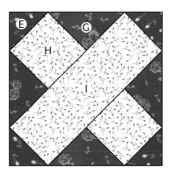

Double Cross Block

MATERIALS

Yardages are based on 42"-wide fabrics.

2¼ yards of green print for blocks, border, and binding*

2⅛ yards of beige print for blocks

1½ yards of red print for blocks, berries, and border*

⅜ yard of red-and-green plaid for Sawtooth Star Variation blocks**

4⅝ yards of backing fabric

58" x 82" piece of batting

Optional: 105 red or burgundy ½"-diameter buttons

The yardage given is enough for borders cut across the width of the fabric. If you prefer to cut lengthwise borders, you'll need 3 yards of green print and 2⅛ yards of red print.

**In the quilt shown the plaid squares are cut on point so that the plaid is on the diagonal. If you wish to do this, you'll need ¾ yard of plaid.*

Cutting for 8 Sawtooth Star Variation Blocks

Fabric	Piece	Number of Strips	Strip Width	First Cut	Second Cut
Green	B	3	3½"	32 squares, 3½" x 3½"	
	D	2	2⅝"	32 squares, 2⅝" x 2⅝"	
Plaid	A	1	6½"	8 squares, 6½" x 6½"	
Beige	B	3	3½"	32 squares, 3½" x 3½"	
	C	2	4¼"	16 squares, 4¼" x 4¼"	Cut all squares ⊠
Red	E	4	3⅞"	32 squares, 3⅞" x 3⅞"	Cut all squares ◩

PIECING THE SAWTOOTH STAR VARIATION BLOCKS

1. Referring to "Quick Corner Triangles" on page 24, position a green B square on the corner of a plaid A square. Stitch, cut, and press. Repeat, stitching a green B square to each corner to give the plaid square four green corners. Make eight.

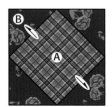

Make 8.

2. Sew beige C triangles to two adjacent sides of a green D square as shown. Make 32. Then sew a red E triangle to each side of these units.

 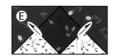

3. Lay out a pieced square from step 1, four pieced rectangles from step 2, and four beige B squares as shown. Sew the units together in rows and then sew the rows together to complete one Sawtooth Star Variation block. Repeat to make all eight blocks.

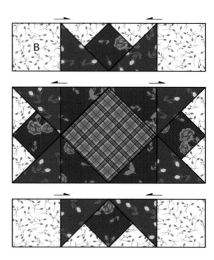

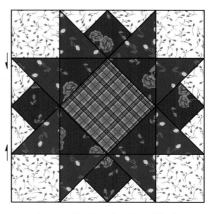

Sawtooth Star Variation Block
Make 8.

Cutting for 7 Double Cross Blocks					
Fabric	**Piece**	**Number of Strips**	**Strip Width**	**First Cut**	**Second Cut**
Green	G	2	7¼"	7 squares, 7¼" x 7¼"	Cut all squares ⊠
Beige	H	2	4¾"	14 squares, 4¾" x 4¾"	
	I	3	4¾"	7 rectangles, 4¾" x 13¼"	
Red	E	2	3⅞"	14 squares, 3⅞" x 3⅞"	Cut all squares ◻

PIECING THE DOUBLE CROSS BLOCKS

1. Sew a green G triangle to opposite sides of a beige H square. Add a red E triangle to the short end of the units as shown. Make 14.

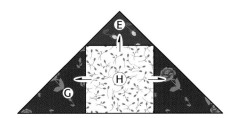

Make 14.

2. Sew red E triangles to opposite ends of the beige I rectangles as shown. Make seven.

Make 7.

3. Sew the large pieced triangles from step 2 to each side of the long units made in step 3. Make seven.

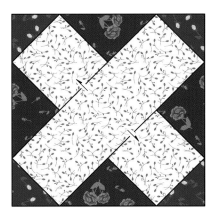

Double Cross Block
Make 7.

ADDING THE APPLIQUÉ

1. Referring to "Appliqué Techniques" on page 12, use the method of your choice to prepare the following number of pieces (patterns on page 56):
   - 14 green vines, cut on the bias, 1⅛" x 12"
   - 28 green leaf 1
   - 28 green leaf 2
   - 28 green leaf 3
   - 105 red berries (or use buttons)

2. Appliqué the vines to the long X-shaped beige spaces in the blocks, using the method of your choice and referring to the appliqué placement diagram. Next, appliqué the A leaves in place, followed by the B leaves, and then the C leaves. Last, appliqué the berries (or stitch the buttons) in place.

Appliqué Placement

Cutting for Borders and Binding

Fabric	Piece	Number of Strips	Strip Width	First Cut	Second Cut
Beige	C	1	4¼"	3 squares, 4¼" x 4¼"	Cut all squares ⊠
	E	Use remainder of 4¼" strip above	3⅞"	2 squares, 3⅞" x 3⅞"	
	G	2	7¼"	8 squares, 7¼" x 7¼"	Cut all squares ⊠
Green	G	1	7¼"	3 squares, 7¼" x 7¼"	Cut all squares ⊠
	D	1	2⅝"	6 squares, 2⅝" x 2⅝"	
	Border 3	7	3½"		
	Binding	7	2¼"		
Red	E	2	3⅞"	18 squares, 3⅞" x 3⅞"	Cut 16 squares ◩
	Border 2	6	1½"		

MAKING THE PIECED BORDER

1. Sew beige C triangles to two adjacent sides of a green D square. Make six.

Make 6.

2. Sew beige G triangles to adjacent sides of the pieced triangles made in step 1. Attach a red E triangle to opposite ends of each unit.

Make 6.

3. Sew beige G triangles to adjacent sides of a green G triangle as shown. Make 10. Add red E triangles to the ends of each unit.

 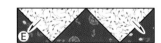

Make 10.

4. Referring to "Half-Square Triangles" on page 23, place a beige E square on a red E square. Stitch, cut, and press. Repeat to make a total of four triangle squares for the border corners.

Make 4.

5. To assemble the top and bottom pieced borders, sew a unit from step 3 to either end of a unit from step 2. Repeat to make a second border. Then sew a triangle square from step 4 to the end of each border. To assemble the side pieced borders, sew three step 3 units to two step 2 units, alternating them as shown.

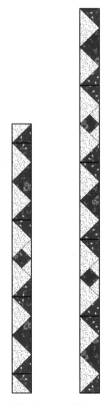

Make 2.   Make 2.

ASSEMBLING THE QUILT TOP

1. Lay out the quilt blocks in five rows of three blocks each, alternating the block designs. Note that the Sawtooth Star Variation blocks should be in the outer corners of the quilt.

2. Sew the blocks together into rows and then join the rows. Press.

3. Sew the longer pieced borders to the sides of the quilt top, taking care to orient them as shown in the quilt assembly diagram below. Press the seam allowances toward the borders. Then, sew the shorter pieced borders to the top and bottom of the quilt.

4. Sew the 1½"-wide red border strips together end to end. From the long strips, cut two borders 48" long and two borders 72" long. Likewise, sew the 3½"-wide green border strips together end to end and from them cut two borders 54" long and two borders 78" long.

5. Matching center points, pin and sew the red and green border strips together lengthwise to make combined borders for each side of the quilt. Referring to "Mitered Corners" on page 25, attach the borders to the quilt top. Miter the corners and press.

FINISHING THE QUILT

Referring to "Finishing the Quilt" on page 27, prepare the backing fabric and then layer the backing, batting, and quilt top. After basting the layers together, hand or machine quilt as desired and then bind your quilt, using the 2¼"-wide green strips.

Quilt Assembly

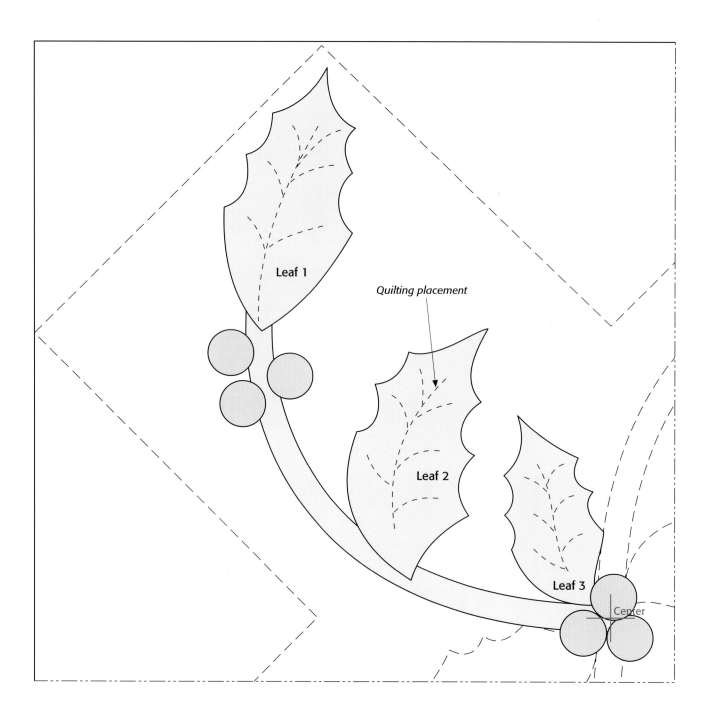

Leaf 1

Quilting placement

Leaf 2

Leaf 3

Center

Appliqué Patterns

Seam allowances are not included.

Designed by Claudia Olson; made by Mary Rozendaal, 2002, Wenatchee, Washington;
machine quilted by Jill Therriault.

Woodland animals are framed in an on-point square of triangles. When the Crow's Foot block is joined with a variation of the Garden Path block, green triangles frame an open area, perfect for appliqué. The green, brown, and dark red colors make a subtle backdrop for woodland animals. The secondary pattern is completed in the border and then given a zigzag frame.

Finished Quilt Size: 85" x 85"
Finished Block Size: 12"

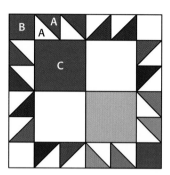

Crow's Foot Block

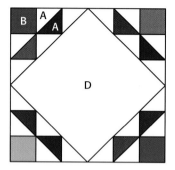

Garden Path Variation Block

MATERIALS

Yardages are based on 42"-wide fabrics.

4 yards total of assorted beige prints for blocks and inner border

2¾ yards total of assorted greens for blocks and pieced borders

1⅜ yards of tan print for outer pieced border

1⅜ yards of green print for outer border and binding*

1⅛ yards total of assorted dark reds and rusts for blocks and pieced border

1 yard total of assorted brown prints for blocks

Assorted scraps of beige, black, brown, dark red, gray, salmon, green, orange, yellow, and white for animal appliqués

5 yards of backing fabric

90" x 90" piece of batting

Embroidery floss or pearl cotton to match fabrics for appliqué

The yardage given is enough for borders cut across the width of the fabric. If you prefer to cut lengthwise borders, you'll need 2¾ yards of green print.

CROW'S PATH VARIATION

Designed by Claudia Olson; made by Pam James, 2001, 76½" x 76½", Cashmere, Washington; machine quilted by Jill Therriault. This version uses several different beige prints and adds gold, which gives the quilt a sparkly effect.

Cutting for 13 Crow's Foot Blocks				
Fabric	Piece	Number of Strips	Strip Width	First Cut
Beiges	A	8	2⅞"	104 squares, 2⅞" x 2⅞"
	B	2	2½"	26 squares, 2½" x 2½"
	C	4	4½"	26 squares, 4½" x 4½"
Assorted greens	A	4	2⅞"	52 squares, 2⅞" x 2⅞"
Browns	A	2	2⅞"	26 squares, 2⅞" x 2⅞"
	C	2	4½"	13 squares, 4½" x 4½"
Dark reds	A	2	2⅞"	26 squares, 2⅞" x 2⅞"
	B	2	2½"	26 squares, 2½" x 2½"
	C	2	4½"	13 squares, 4½" x 4½"

PIECING THE CROW'S FOOT BLOCKS

1. Referring to "Half-Square Triangles" on page 23, position a beige A square on a green A square. Stitch, cut, and press. Make 52 to yield 104 beige/green triangle squares. Repeat to make brown/beige as well as red/beige triangle squares. Make 26 of these two combinations to yield 52 triangle squares each.

Make 104.   Make 52.   Make 52.

2. Sew the green triangle squares together in pairs as shown. Notice that the direction of the triangles changes for half of the pairs. Make 26 of each.

Make 26 each.

3. Repeat step 2 to join pairs of brown triangle squares and pairs of red triangle squares as shown. Again, note that the direction of the triangles changes for half of the pairs. Make 13 of each color in each direction.

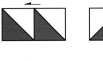

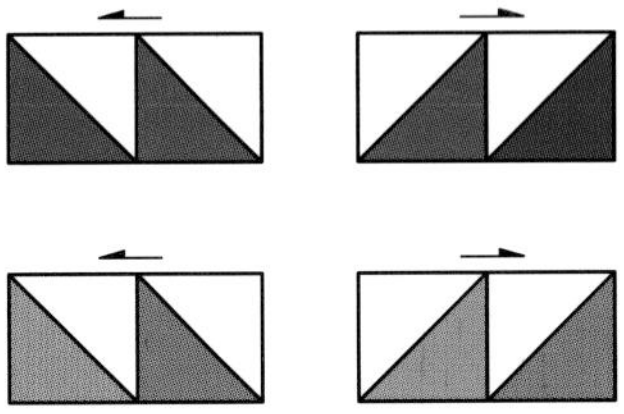

Make 13 each.

4. Lay out the pairs of green triangle squares with beige B and C squares as shown. Sew the units together in rows and then join the rows to complete a quarter block. Make 26.

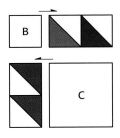 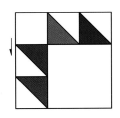

Make 26.

5. Repeat step 4, this time using the pairs of brown triangle squares, a red B square, and a brown C square. Make 13. In the same manner, make 13 quarter blocks using the red triangle squares with red B and C squares.

6. Lay out the quarter blocks or "feet" as shown to make one block. You'll need one brown foot, one red foot, and two green feet per block. Sew the units together in rows and then join the rows. Press. Make a total of 13 Crow's Foot blocks.

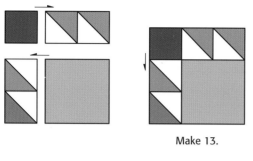
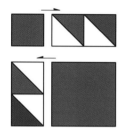

Make 13.

Make 13.

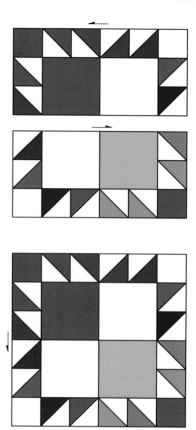

Crow's Foot Block
Make 13.

		Cutting for 12 Garden Path Variation Blocks			
Fabric	Piece	Number of Strips	Strip Width	First Cut	Second Cut
Beiges	D	3	9½"	12 squares, 9½" x 9½"	
	A	10	2⅞"	120 squares, 2⅞" x 2⅞"	Cut 72 of the squares ◺
Assorted greens	A	4	2⅞"	48 squares, 2⅞" x 2⅞"	
Dark reds	B	2	2½"	24 squares, 2½" x 2½"	
Browns	B	2	2½"	24 squares, 2½" x 2½"	

MAKING THE GARDEN PATH VARIATION BLOCKS

1. Referring to "Appliqué Techniques" on page 12, use the method of your choice to prepare the animal shapes (patterns on pages 66–70). Note that there are two of the bear block; one is made with the pattern reversed.

    Appliqué each animal to a beige D square. Do not appliqué antlers on the elk, deer, or moose until block piecing is completed, since they extend beyond the center square. Trim the completed appliquéd squares to 9" x 9", being careful to center the animals within the squares.

2. Referring to "Half-Square Triangles" on page 23, position a beige A square on a green A square. Stitch, cut, and press. Make 48 to yield 96 triangle squares.

Make 96.

3. Sew a beige A triangle to one green side of each triangle square as shown. Make 96. To 48 of the units, sew another beige A triangle to the adjacent green side.

Make 48.

4. Sew a red B square to the ends of half of the units created in the first part of step 3. Sew a brown B square to the other half. Make 24 of each.

Make 24 each.

5. Join the units from steps 3 and 4 to make large pieced corner triangles. You will have 24 with a red corner square and 24 with a brown corner square.

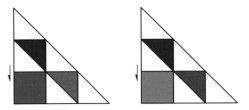

Make 24 each.

6. Attach the pieced corner triangles with red corner squares to the top left and bottom right of the appliquéd squares. Sew the corner triangles with brown corner squares to the remaining sides. Color placement of the red and brown squares is important, as these squares will form a four-patch design when the blocks are joined with the Crow's Foot blocks. Repeat to make 12 blocks.

Garden Path Variation Block
Make 12.

7. Finish appliquéing any animal parts that extend beyond the center square.

Cutting for Borders and Binding

Note: To cut the 3⁵⁄₁₆" squares, measure midway between the 3¼" and 3⅜" markings on your ruler.

Fabric	Piece	Number of Strips	Strip Width	First Cut	Second Cut
Beiges	A	Use remainder of 2⅞" strip from Garden Path Variation blocks	2⅞"	2 squares, 2⅞" x 2⅞"	Cut all squares ◻
	B	2	2½"	32 squares, 2½" x 2½"	
	E	3	4⅞"	20 squares, 4⅞" x 4⅞"	
	F	1	2½"	8 rectangles, 2½" x 4½"	
	G	2	2½"	8 rectangles, 2½" x 8½"	
Assorted greens	B	1	2½"	8 squares, 2½" x 2½"	
	E	3	4⅞"	20 squares, 4⅞" x 4⅞"	
	F	1	2½"	8 rectangles, 2½" x 4½"	
	H	9	4½"	72 squares, 4½" x 4½"	
	J	1	5¼"	2 squares, 5¼" x 5¼"	Cut all squares ⊠
	I	Use remainder of 5¼" strip above	3⁵⁄₁₆"	4 squares, 3⁵⁄₁₆" x 3⁵⁄₁₆"	
Tan	B	1	2½"	8 squares, 2½" x 2½"	
	G	2	8½"	32 rectangles, 2½" x 8½"	
	K	1	2½"	4 rectangles, 2½" x 6½"	
Dark reds	A	1	2⅞"	2 squares, 2⅞" x 2⅞"	Cut all squares ◻
	G	2	8½"	28 rectangles, 2½" x 8½"	
	J	1	5¼"	2 squares, 5¼" x 5¼"	Cut all squares ⊠
Darker assorted greens	I	1	3⁵⁄₁₆"	4 squares, 3⁵⁄₁₆" x 3⁵⁄₁₆"	
Green print	Outer border	9	2½"		
	Binding	9	2¼"		

PIECING THE INNER BORDER

1. Referring to "Half-Square Triangles" on page 23, position a beige E square on a green E square. Stitch, cut, and press. Make 20 to yield 40 triangle squares. Join triangle squares to form 12 pairs as shown. Reserve the remaining triangle squares for later.

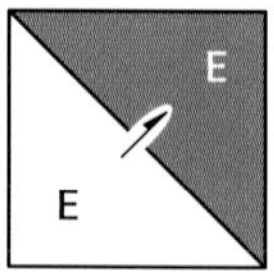

2. Referring to "Quick Corner Triangles" on page 24, position a green B square on the end of a beige F rectangle. Draw the diagonal line from top right to bottom left. Stitch, cut and press. Make four of these left units. Repeat, this time sewing from top left to bottom right on the squares to make four right units.

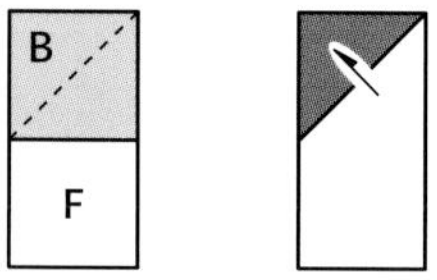

Make 40.

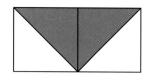

Make 12.

Make 4.

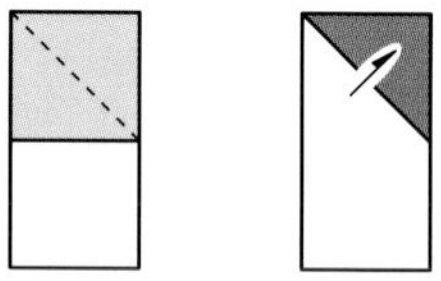

Make 4.

3. Sew each pieced rectangle from step 2 to a pair of triangle squares from step 1, positioning them as shown. Make four of each.

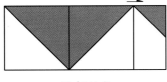

Left Unit
Make 4.

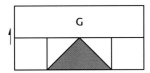

Right Unit
Make 4.

4. Using the quick-corner-triangles technique, position a beige B square on the end of a green F rectangle. Stitch, cut, and press. In the same manner, position another beige B square on the other end of the green rectangle to make a flying-geese unit. Stitch, cut and press. Make eight. Sew a beige B square on each end of the flying-geese units.

Make 8.

5. Sew a beige G rectangle to the top of the units made in step 4 as shown.

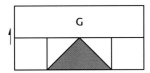

6. Using the technique for quick corner triangles, position a green H square on the end of the units made in step 5. Stitch, cut, and press. In the same manner, position another green H square on the

other end of the unit to make another green corner. Stitch, cut and press. Make eight.

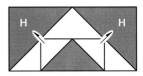

7. Sew triangle squares from step 1 to the ends of the units made in step 6 as shown.

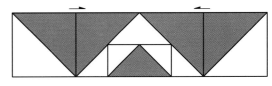

Make 8.

8. Using a single pair of triangle squares (reserved from step 1), two units from step 7, and a left and a right unit from step 2, assemble one inner border as shown. Repeat to make a total of four inner borders.

Inner Border
Make 4.

PIECING THE OUTER BORDER

1. Sew a tan G rectangle to a dark red G rectangle as shown. Make 28.

2. Using the technique for quick corner triangles, position a green H square on the end of the unit made in step 1. Stitch, cut, and press. Repeat, sewing a green H square to the other end to make a flying-geese unit. Make 28.

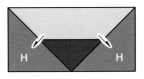

Make 28.

3. Using the quick-corner-triangles technique, position a tan B square on the end of a green F rectangle. Stitch diagonally from the top right to bottom left, cut, and press to make a left unit. Make four. Repeat, this time sewing the squares diagonally from top left to bottom right to make four right units.

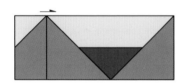

Left Unit
Make 4.   Right Unit
Make 4.

4. Sew the left pieced rectangles from step 3 to the left side of four flying-geese units from step 2 as shown. Repeat, sewing the right pieced rectangles to the right side of four other flying-geese units.

Left Unit
Make 4.

Right Unit
Make 4.

5. To assemble a border, join five flying-geese units from step 2. Add a right and left unit to opposite ends of the border as shown. Repeat to make a total of four outer borders.

Outer Border
Make 4.

PIECING THE BORDER CORNERS

1. Sew a dark red A triangle to a darker green I square. Make four. Join dark red J triangles to opposite sides of each unit as shown.

Make 4.

2. Sew a beige A triangle to a green I square. Make four. Join green J triangles to opposite sides of each unit as shown.

Make 4.

3. Join the pieced triangles from step 1 to those made in step 2. Then sew a tan K rectangle to the top of the pieced square followed by a tan G rectangle to the left side of the pieced square as shown to complete the border corner. Make four.

Border Corner
Make 4.

ASSEMBLING THE QUILT TOP

1. Referring to the quilt assembly diagram opposite, lay out the quilt blocks in five rows of five blocks each, starting with a Crow's Foot block in the upper right corner and alternating with Garden Path Variation blocks as you go. Sew the blocks together into rows and then join the rows.

2. Sew each pieced inner border to a pieced outer border as shown. Press the seam allowances toward the inner border.

3. Sew a pieced border to opposite sides of the quilt top. Then sew a border corner to the remaining two pieced borders and sew them to the top and bottom of the quilt. Press the seam allowances toward the border.

4. Join the nine 1½"-wide green print border strips together end to end. From them, cut four border strips, each 90" long. Referring to "Squared Corners" on page 25, measure, pin, and sew the green borders to the quilt top.

FINISHING THE QUILT

Referring to "Finishing the Quilt" on page 27, prepare the backing fabric and then layer the backing, batting, and quilt top. After basting the layers together, hand or machine quilt as desired and then bind your quilt, using the 2¼"-wide green print strips.

Quilt Assembly

Appliqué Patterns

Enlarge patterns 133%.
Embroider details as indicated.

▨▨▨ Satin stitch

········ Stem stitch

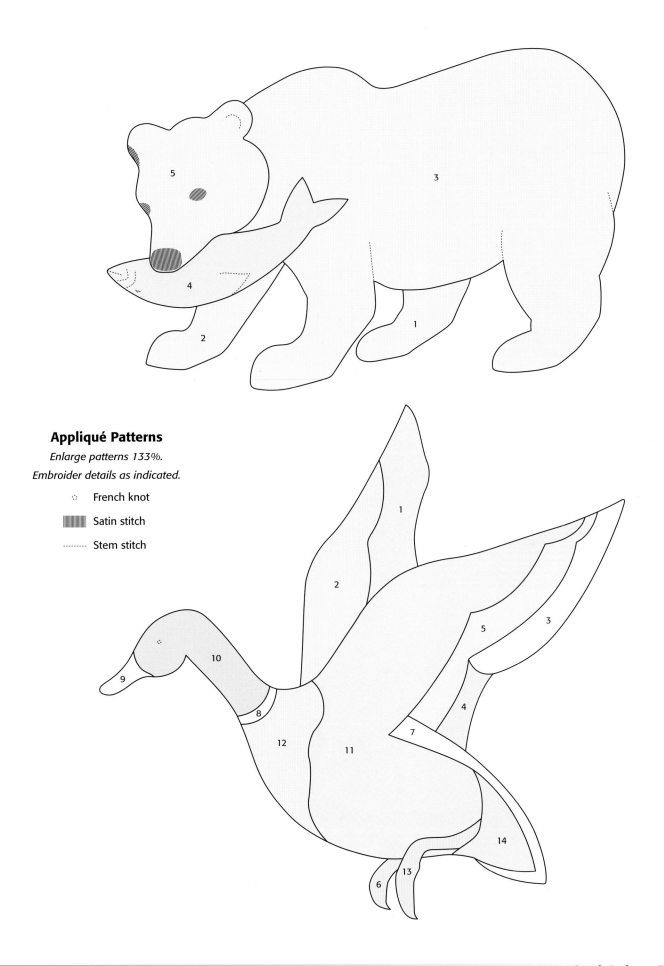

Appliqué Patterns

Enlarge patterns 133%.

Embroider details as indicated.

⊙   French knot

▓▓▓   Satin stitch

·······   Stem stitch

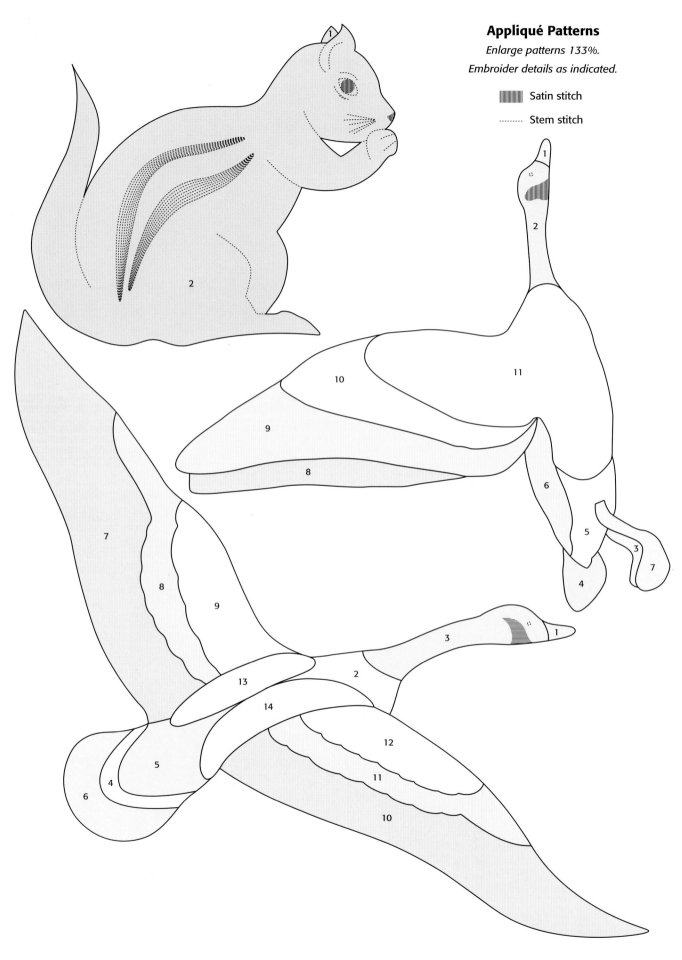

Appliqué Patterns

Enlarge patterns 133%.

Embroider details as indicated.

▓▓▓ Satin stitch

········ Stem stitch

Appliqué Patterns

Enlarge patterns 133%.
Embroider details as indicated.

▦ Satin stitch
········ Stem stitch

Appliqué Patterns

Enlarge patterns 133%.

Embroider details as indicated.

▓▓▓▓▓ Satin stitch

······ Stem stitch

Feathered Flowers

Designed, made, and hand quilted by Claudia Olson, 2003, Wenatchee, Washington.

This quilt is a little bit different from the others in the book because it doesn't use two different pieced blocks. Instead, I used several variations of a pieced block called Cobblestones. The variations among the Cobblestones blocks let me set the blocks together to make red and purple feathered stars appear around each appliquéd block. I appliquéd purple and red flowers with green vines and leaves and surrounded the pieced stars with an appliquéd vine. In addition to plenty of space for appliqué, this quilt also has lots of space to show off fine quilting.

Finished Quilt Size: 76" x 76"
Finished Block Size: 16"

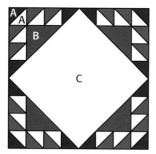

Cobblestones Block

Fantasy Flower Block

MATERIALS

Yardages are based on 42"-wide fabrics.

5½ yards of beige solid for block backgrounds and piecing

1 yard of green print for appliqués

1 yard of medium purple print 1 for blocks and appliqués

¾ yard of dark purple print for blocks and border

¼ yard of medium purple print 2 for appliqués

⅛ yard of medium purple print 3 for appliqués

2 yards of red print 1 for patchwork, appliqués, border, and binding*

¼ yard of red print 2 for appliqués

⅜ yard of red print 3 for appliqués

⅛ yard of red print 4 for appliqués

⅛ yard of brown print for appliqués

4⅔ yards of backing fabric

83" x 83" piece of batting

The yardage given is enough for borders cut across the width of the fabric. If you prefer to cut lengthwise borders, you'll need 2⅓ yards of red print 1.

Cutting for 5 Cobblestones Blocks and 4 Half Blocks

Note: *To cut the 11¹³⁄₁₆" squares, measure midway between the 11¾" and 11⅞" markings on your ruler.*

Fabric	Piece	Number of Strips	Strip Width	First Cut	Second Cut
Beige	A	5	2⅞"	60 squares, 2⅞" x 2⅞"	
	C	2	11¹³⁄₁₆"	5 squares, 11¹³⁄₁₆" x 11¹³⁄₁₆"	
	D	1	8⅞"	2 squares, 8⅞" x 8⅞"	Cut all squares ◻
	E	1	17¼"	1 square, 17¼" x 17¼"	Cut square ⊠
Medium purple 1	A	4	2⅞"	48 squares, 2⅞" x 2⅞"	
Dark purple	A	2	2⅞"	24 squares, 2⅞" x 2⅞"	Cut 12 squares ◻
Red 1	B	2	4⅞"	12 squares, 4⅞" x 4⅞"	Cut all squares ◻

PIECING THE COBBLESTONES BLOCKS

Make one block with four pieced corners and four blocks with three pieced and one plain corner. In addition, make four half Cobblestones blocks.

1. Referring to "Half-Square Triangles" on page 23, position a beige A square on a medium purple A square. Stitch, cut, and press. Make 48 to yield 96 triangle squares. In the same manner, use beige and dark purple A squares to sew 12 units to yield 24 triangle squares.

Make 96.   Make 24.

2. Sew the medium purple triangle squares together in pairs with half the pairs facing one way and half facing the other way as shown.

Make 24
left-facing units.

Make 24
right-facing units.

3. Sew a red B triangle to the left-facing pairs of triangle squares as shown. Sew a dark purple triangle square from step 1 to the right side of the right-facing pairs as shown.

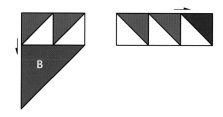

4. Sew together the units made in step 3. Then join dark purple A triangles to the ends of each beige triangle to complete a large pieced triangle. Make 24.

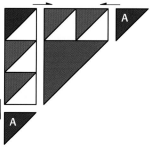

Make 24.

5. Sew a large pieced triangle to opposite ends of a beige C square. Make five.

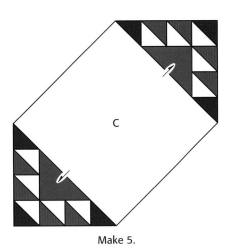

Make 5.

6. Sew pieced triangles to the remaining two sides of one beige square. Sew one pieced triangle and one beige D triangle to the remaining two sides of the four other blocks.

Make 1.

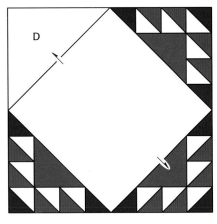

Make 4.

7. Sew the remaining large pieced triangles from the Cobblestones blocks to the short sides of the beige E triangles. Make four half Cobblestones blocks. Reserve for the pieced border units.

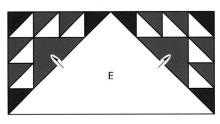

Make 4.

MAKING THE APPLIQUÉ BLOCKS

1. From the beige fabric, cut four appliqué backgrounds 17½" x 17½". Turn under or serge the edges of the squares.

2. Referring to "Appliqué Techniques" on page 12, use the method of your choice to prepare the appliqué shapes (patterns on page 78) for four Fantasy Flower blocks. Note that there are three different flowers; each flower appears four times per block (two times in reverse). Therefore, to complete all four blocks, you will need to prepare eight of each flower petal and eight of each flower petal reversed. You will need to make eight of each leaf and eight of each leaf reversed.

   In addition, make 32 berries, 36 of leaf 3, and 36 of leaf 3 reversed for the border appliqué. In the quilt shown, flowers 1 and 2, the buds, and the berries are made from the red fabrics, and flowers 3 and 4 are made from the purple fabrics. All vines and leaves are made from the green print. Appliqué each block in numerical order as indicated on the patterns.

3. Trim the completed blocks to 16½" x 16½", taking care to keep the appliqué designs centered within the blocks.

Cutting for Border and Binding					
Fabric	**Piece**	**Number of Strips**	**Strip Width**	**First Cut**	**Second Cut**
Beige	B	1	4⅞"	16 squares, 4⅞" x 4⅞"	Cut all squares ⧅
	D	1	8½"	4 squares, 8½" x 8½"	
	F	1	8⅞"	2 squares, 8⅞" x 8⅞"	Cut all squares ⧅
	I	4	8½"	8 rectangles, 8½" x 16½"	
	J	1	9¼"	3 squares, 9¼" x 9¼"	Cut all squares ⊠
	K	4	2½"	64 squares, 2½" x 2½"	
Red 1	G	2	4½"	32 rectangles, 2½" x 4½"	
	Border	8	2½"		
	Binding	8	2¼"		
Medium purple 1	A	3	2⅞"	32 squares, 2⅞" x 2⅞"	Cut all squares ⧅
Dark purple	H	2	5¼"	8 squares, 5¼" x 5¼"	Cut all squares ⊠

Piecing the Border Units

1. Referring to "Quick Corner Triangles" on page 24, position a beige F square on the end of a red G rectangle. Stitch, cut, and press. Repeat, adding a beige corner on the other end of the rectangle to make a flying-geese unit. Make 32.

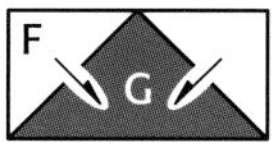

Make 32.

2. Sew a medium purple A triangle to each end of the units made in step 1 as shown. Then join a dark purple H triangle to the top of each unit. Make 32 large pieced triangles.

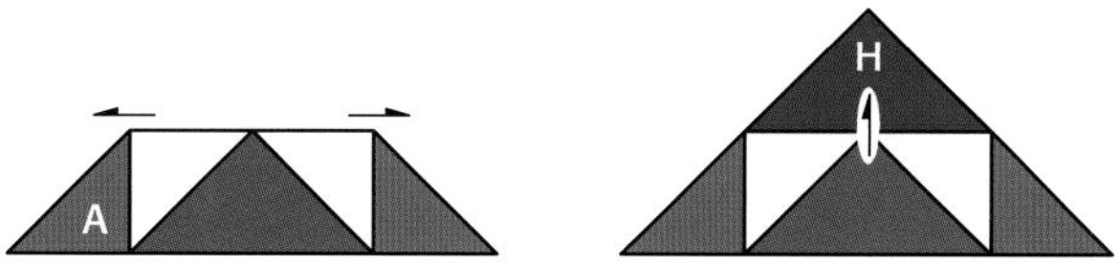

Make 32.

3. Sew a beige B triangle to one side of each pieced triangle made in step 2; sew 16 with the beige triangle on the left and 16 with the beige triangle on the right. Then join the two types of units to either side of the beige I triangles. Make 12.

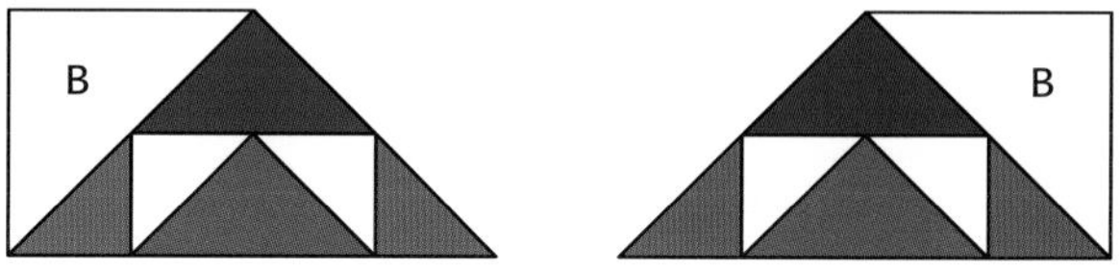

Make 16. Make 16.

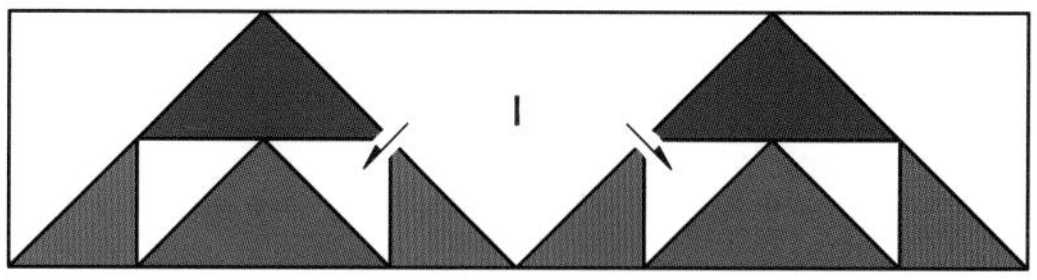

Make 12.

4. Sew a double-triangle unit from step 3 to a beige J rectangle as shown. Make eight, reserving the remaining four double-triangle units for the next step.

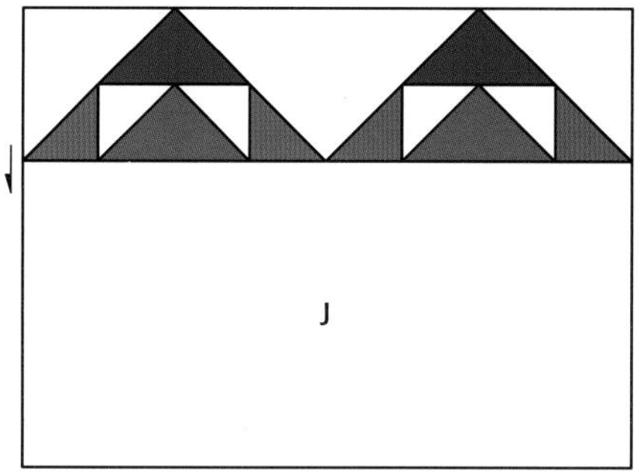

Make 8.

5. Sew the remaining double-triangle units to the half Cobblestones blocks made in step 7 on page 74 as shown. Make four.

Make 4.

6. Sew the pieced triangles reserved from step 3 to adjacent sides of a beige K square as shown. Attach a beige D triangle to the unit to make a border corner square. Make four.

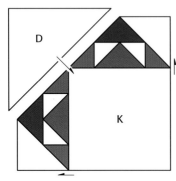

Make 4.

ASSEMBLING THE QUILT TOP

1. Lay out the quilt blocks and border units in five rows as shown. Note that rows 1 and 5 are mirror images of one another, as are rows 2 and 4.

2. Sew the blocks and units together in rows, pressing seam allowances away from the appliqué blocks. Join the rows.

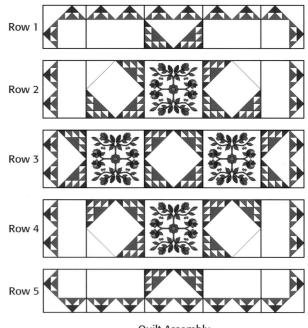

Quilt Assembly

3. Using the flower 4 and leaf 3 patterns on page 78, prepare 4 flowers and 72 leaves for appliqué. You will also need to make eight sections of bias stems, each finishing ¼" wide by approximately 18" long. In the quilt shown, the corner flowers are made from red print 2, and the leaves and vines are made from the green print. Refer to the quilt photograph on page 71 and the illustration below for appliqué placement.

Appliqué Placement Guide

4. Sew the 2½"-wide red border strips together, end to end, in pairs to make four border strips approximately 80" long. Referring to "Mitered Corners" on page 25, measure, pin, and sew the border strips to the quilt top, mitering the corners.

FINISHING THE QUILT

Referring to "Finishing the Quilt" on page 27, prepare the backing fabric and then layer the backing, batting, and quilt top. After basting the layers together, hand or machine quilt as desired and then bind your quilt, using the 2¼"-wide red strips.

Quilt Plan

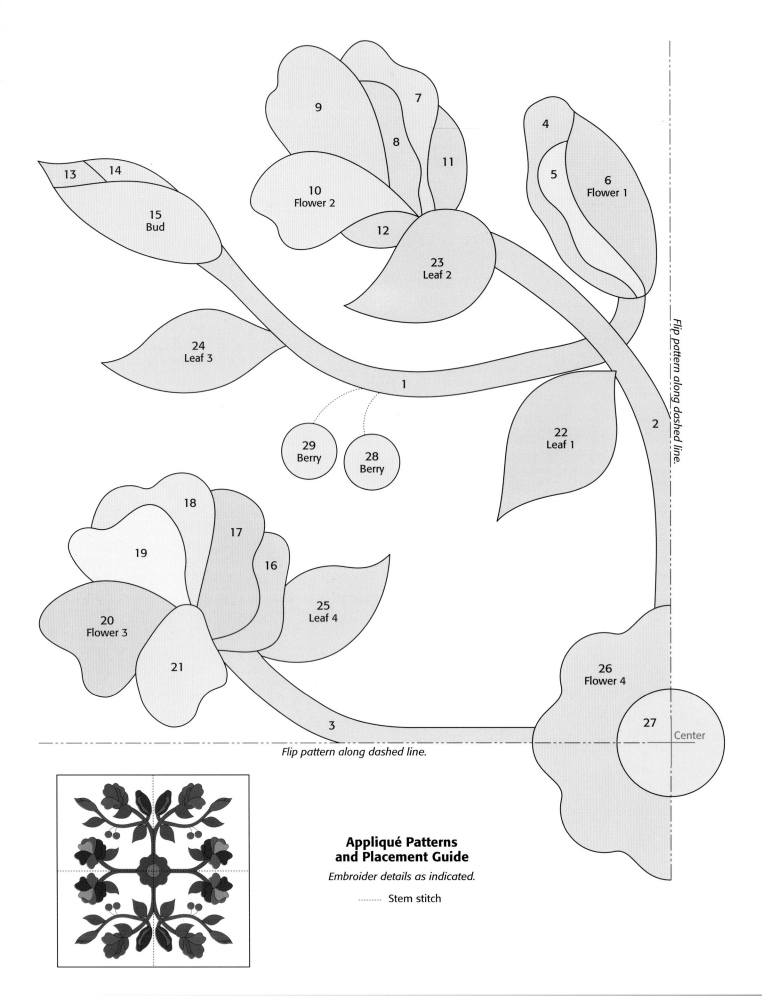

Flip pattern along dashed line.

9

7

8

11

4

5

6
Flower 1

13 14

15
Bud

10
Flower 2

12

23
Leaf 2

24
Leaf 3

1

22
Leaf 1

2

29
Berry

28
Berry

18

17

19

16

20
Flower 3

25
Leaf 4

21

3

26
Flower 4

27

Center

Flip pattern along dashed line.

**Appliqué Patterns
and Placement Guide**

Embroider details as indicated.

········· Stem stitch

Designed and made by Claudia Olson, 2001, Wenatchee, Washington; machine quilted by Jill Therriault.

"Folk-Art Stars" is made using Ohio Star blocks and Mosaic Variation blocks. While overall the colors of the blocks are soft, I kept the triangles that frame the folk-art animals and garden motifs dark to concentrate the focus on the appliqué. I used light plaids for the star points to create an interesting pieced background for the quilt that wouldn't detract attention from the appliqué. The simplicity of muslin and a wide variety of plaids adds to the charm of this easygoing quilt.

Finished Quilt Size: 72½" x 72½"
Finished Block Size: 12"

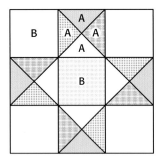

Ohio Star Block

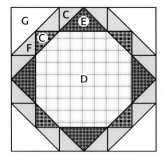

Mosaic Variation Block

MATERIALS

Yardages are based on 42"-wide fabrics.

¾ yard total of assorted dark plaids for blocks

1⅞ yards of muslin for blocks

1¾ yards of dark plaid for outer border and binding*

1½ yards of tan print for blocks and pieced border

1 yard total of assorted light plaids for blocks

⅞ yard total of light beige prints or plaids for Mosaic Variation blocks

¾ yard of medium blue plaid for inner border

Scraps of assorted reds, blues, browns, golds, oranges, terra cottas, blacks, grays, and greens for appliqués

4½ yards of backing fabric

77" x 77" piece of batting

Assorted embroidery flosses

The yardage given is enough for borders cut across the width of the fabric. If you prefer to cut lengthwise borders, you'll need 2⅜ yards of dark plaid.

Cutting for 13 Ohio Star Blocks

Fabric	Piece	Number of Strips	Strip Width	First Cut
Muslin	A	2	5¼"	13 squares, 5¼" x 5¼"
	B	7	4½"	52 squares, 4½" x 4½"
Light plaids	A	4	5¼"	26 squares, 5¼" x 5¼"
	B	2	4½"	13 squares, 4½" x 4½"
Tan	A	2	5¼"	13 squares, 5¼" x 5¼"

PIECING THE OHIO STAR BLOCKS

1. Referring to "Quarter Square Triangles" on page 23, position a muslin A square on a light plaid A square. Stitch on the right side of the drawn lines, cut, and press. Repeat, stitching a total of 13 pairs of squares to yield 52 triangle pairs with the plaid fabrics on the right.

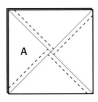

Make 52.

2. Repeat step 1, using tan A squares and assorted light plaid A squares. Make 13 to yield 52 triangle pairs with the plaid on the right.

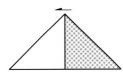

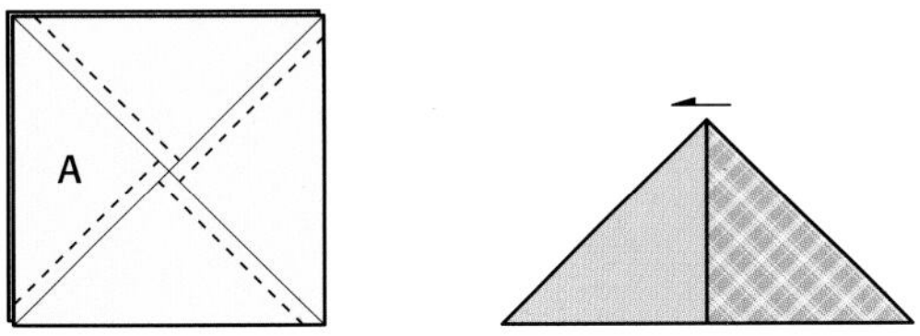

Make 52.

3. Sew the triangle pairs from step 1 to the triangle pairs from step 2 as shown. Make four matching hourglass units, then continue sewing the pairs together so that you have 13 sets of four identical hourglass units.

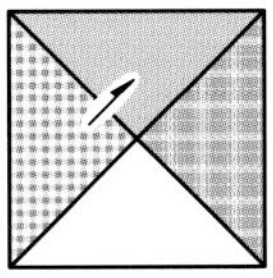

Make 52.

4. Lay out four matching hourglass units with four muslin B squares and one light plaid B square as shown. Make sure that the muslin triangles are all facing the center of the block. Sew the pieces together in rows and then join the rows to complete an Ohio Star block. Repeat to make 13 blocks.

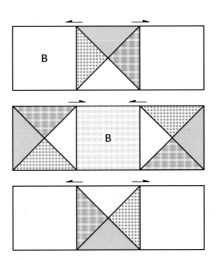

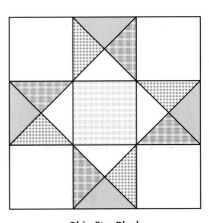

Ohio Star Block
Make 13.

Cutting for 12 Mosaic Variation Blocks

Fabric	Piece	Number of Strips	Strip Width	First Cut	Second Cut
Assorted dark plaids	C	3	2½"	48 squares, 2½" x 2½"	
	E	3	4½"	48 rectangles, 2½" x 4½"	
Light beiges	D	3	8½"	12 squares, 8½" x 8½"	
Tan	F	4	2⅞"	48 squares, 2⅞" x 2⅞"	Cut all squares ◩
	C	6	2½"	96 squares, 2½" x 2½"	
Muslin	G	3	4⅞"	24 squares, 4⅞" x 4⅞"	Cut all squares ◩

PIECING THE MOSAIC VARIATION BLOCKS

1. Referring to "Quick Corner Triangles" on page 24, sew matching dark plaid C squares to each corner of a light beige D square. Repeat, making 12 blocks.

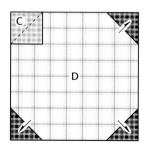

Make 12.

2. Using the technique for quick corner triangles, sew a tan C square to the corner of a dark plaid E rectangle. Repeat, sewing a matching tan C square to the other end of the rectangle to make a flying-geese unit. Make four matching units. Repeat, making a total of 48 flying-geese units in sets of four matching units. Then sew a tan F triangle to opposite ends of each flying-geese unit.

 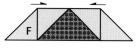

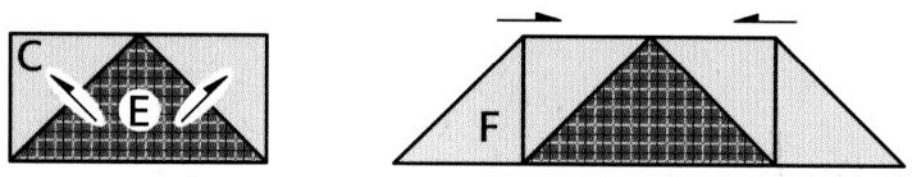

Make 48.

3. Select four matching units from step 2 and sew one to each side of a large pieced square from step 1 as shown. Repeat for all 12 blocks.

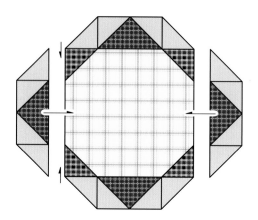

4. Sew a muslin G triangle to each corner of the blocks to complete 12 Mosaic Variation blocks.

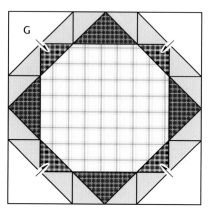

Mosaic Variation Block
Make 12.

Adding the Appliqué

Referring to "Appliqué Techniques" on page 12, use the method of your choice to prepare the animal, plant, and garden shapes (patterns on pages 85–89).

Appliqué one pattern in the center of each Mosaic variation block. In the quilt shown, the motifs were embroidered with a blanket stitch and embellished with embroidery floss or pearl cotton.

Cutting for Borders and Binding				
Fabric	**Piece**	**Number of Strips**	**Strip Width**	**First Cut**
Tan	C	3	2½"	40 squares, 2½" x 2½"
Medium blue plaid	H	8	2½"	24 rectangles, 2½" x 12½"
Dark plaid	Border	8	4½"	
	Binding	8	2¼"	

Making the Pieced Border

1. Using the technique for quick corner triangles, sew tan C squares to opposite corners of a medium blue plaid H rectangle as shown. Make 16. Then make four rectangles with a tan corner on the right only and four with the tan corner on the left only.

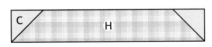

Make 16.

Make 4.

Make 4.

2. Sew four rectangles with two tan corners together end to end. Join a rectangle with a right corner to the left end of the strip and vice versa as shown. The completed border should not have tan triangles on the ends. Repeat to make four of these pieced inner borders.

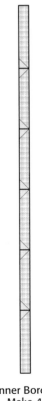

Inner Border
Make 4.

ASSEMBLING THE QUILT TOP

1. Lay out the Ohio Star and Mosaic Variation blocks in five rows of five blocks each. Alternate the block designs, beginning with an Ohio Star block at the top right corner.
2. Sew the blocks together in rows, and then join the rows.
3. Matching seams where possible, sew pieced borders to opposite sides of the quilt top, keeping the tan triangles pointing away from the quilt top. Stop sewing ¼" from the quilt-top edge and allow the extra medium blue plaid fabric to hang over the edge of the quilt top.
4. Sew the remaining two pieced borders to the top and bottom of the quilt in the same fashion.

5. Sew the dark plaid 4½"-wide strips together end to end in pairs to make four border strips. Referring to "Mitered Corners" on page 25, measure, match centers, pin, and sew the dark plaid border strips to the pieced borders. Miter the corners of the double border.

FINISHING THE QUILT

Referring to "Finishing the Quilt" on page 27, prepare the backing fabric and then layer the backing, batting, and quilt top. After basting the layers together, hand or machine quilt as desired and then bind your quilt, using the 2¼"-wide dark plaid strips.

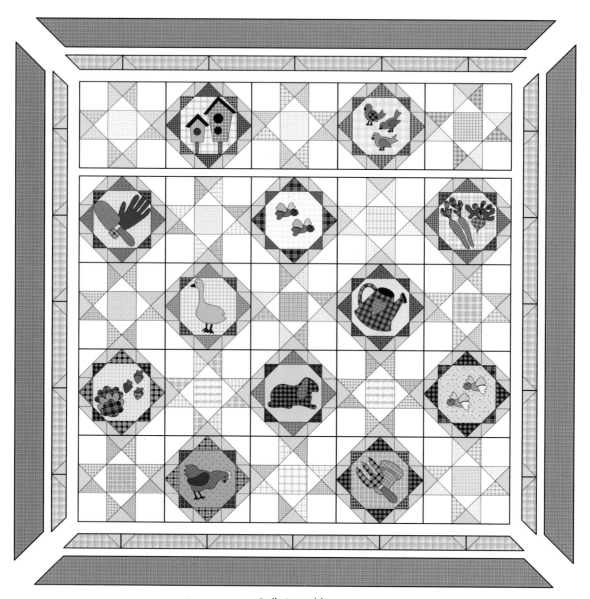

Quilt Assembly

Appliqué Patterns

Enlarge patterns 125%.
Embroider details as indicated.

▓▓▓▓ Satin stitch

Appliqué Patterns

Enlarge patterns 125%.
Embroider details as indicated.

▓▓▓▓▓ Satin stitch

Appliqué Patterns

Enlarge patterns 125%.
Embroider details as indicated.

||||||||| Satin stitch

Appliqué Patterns

Enlarge patterns 125%.

Embroider details as indicated.

▌▌▌▌ Satin stitch

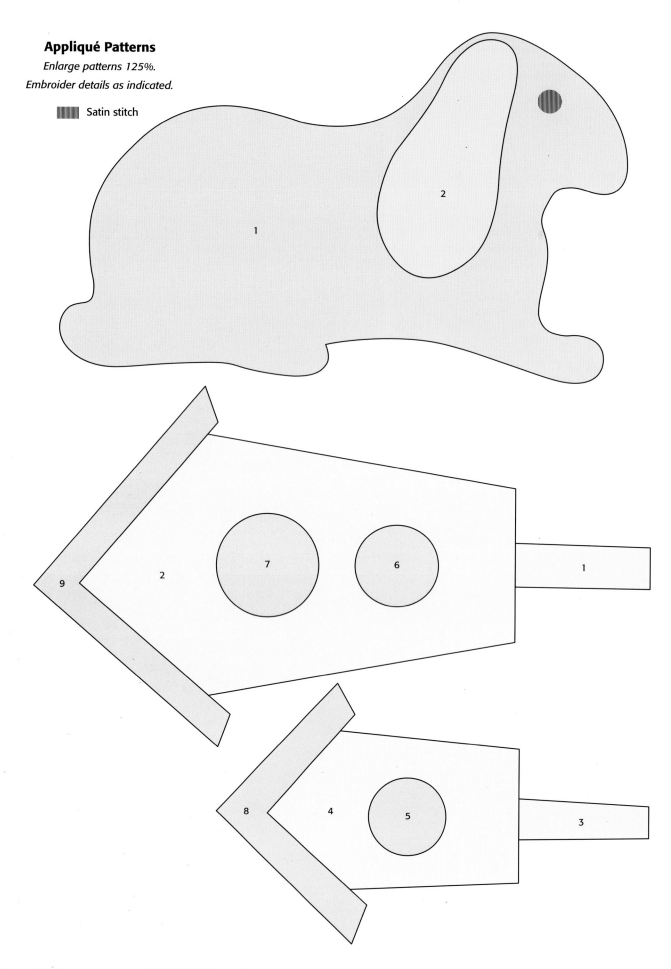

Gentleman's Garden

Designed by Claudia Olson; made and machine quilted by Terry Vaughn, 2001, East Wenatchee, Washington.

"Gentleman's Garden" is made using Gentleman's Fancy blocks and a variation of the Garden Path block. The red triangles surrounding the Garden Path Variation blocks create a broken secondary square. Also, the large mauve and beige triangles form a secondary star pattern. Terry Vaughn's beautifully appliquéd red and gold flowers are striking on the beige backgrounds.

Finished Quilt Size: 50¼" x 50¼"
Finished Block Size: 12"

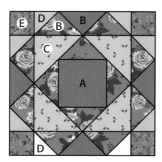

Gentleman's Fancy Block

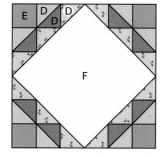

Garden Path Variation Block

MATERIALS

Yardages are based on 42"-wide fabrics.

2 yards of large-scale green floral for Gentleman's Fancy blocks, border, and binding*

⅞ yard of cream print for appliqué backgrounds and center star points

¾ yard of red print for blocks

½ yard of tan print for blocks

½ yard of pink print for blocks

⅜ yard of brown print for Garden Path Variation blocks

⅛ yard of small-scale green print for Gentleman's Fancy blocks

Scraps of reds, pinks, browns, golds, and greens for appliqués

3¼ yards of backing fabric

56" x 56" piece of batting

Gold embroidery floss

Pigma pens to match scraps

The yardage given is enough for borders cut across the width of the fabric. If you prefer to cut lengthwise borders, you'll need 2¼ yards of large-scale green floral.

Cutting for 4 Gentleman's Fancy Blocks

Fabric	Piece	Number of Strips	Strip Width	First Cut	Second Cut
Green floral	B	2	5¼"	12 squares, 5¼" x 5¼"	Cut all squares ⊠
Red	A	1	4½"	4 squares, 4½" x 4½"	
	B	1	5¼"	4 squares, 5¼" x 5¼"	Cut all squares ⊠
Tan	C	1	4⅞"	8 squares, 4⅞" x 4⅞"	Cut all squares ◻
Pink	D	1	2⅞"	12 squares, 2⅞" x 2⅞"	Cut all squares ◻
Cream	D	1	2⅞"	4 squares, 2⅞" x 2⅞"	Cut all squares ◻
Green print	E	1	2½"	16 squares, 2½" x 2½"	

PIECING THE GENTLEMAN'S FANCY BLOCKS

1. Sew green floral B triangles to opposite sides of a red A square as shown. Sew green floral B triangles to the two remaining sides of the red square. Repeat to make four units.

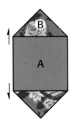

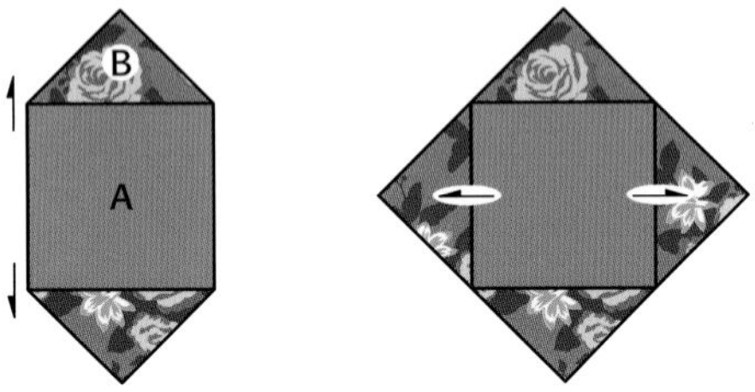

Make 4.

2. In the same manner, sew tan C triangles to all sides of the units from step 1.

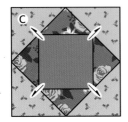

3. Sew green floral B triangles on adjacent sides of a red B triangle as shown. Make 16. To 12 of the units, sew pink D triangles to each end as shown. To the remaining four units, sew cream D triangles.

Make 12.

Make 4.

4. Add a green print E square to the ends of eight of the units with pink triangles.

Make 8.

5. Sew the remaining units with pink triangles to the tops of the pieced square units from step 2. Sew the units with cream triangles to the bottoms of these squares. Finally, attach the units from step 4 to the sides of these blocks to complete four Gentleman's Fancy blocks.

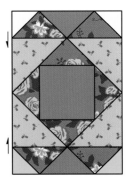

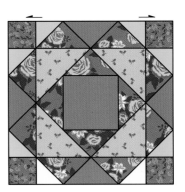

Gentleman's Fancy Block
Make 4.

Cutting for 5 Garden Path Variation Blocks

Fabric	Piece	Number of Strips	Strip Width	First Cut	Second Cut
Pink	D	2	2⅞"	16 squares, 2⅞" x 2⅞"	
Red	D	2	2⅞"	20 squares, 2⅞" x 2⅞"	
Tan	D	3	2⅞"	30 squares, 2⅞" x 2⅞"	Cut all squares ◺
Brown	E	2	2½"	20 squares, 2½" x 2½"	
Cream	D	1	2⅞"	4 squares, 2⅞" x 2⅞"	
	F	2	9"	5 squares, 9" x 9"	

MAKING THE GARDEN PATH VARIATION BLOCKS

1. Referring to "Half-Square Triangles" on page 23, position a pink D square on a red D square. Stitch, cut, and press. Make 16 to yield 32 triangle squares.

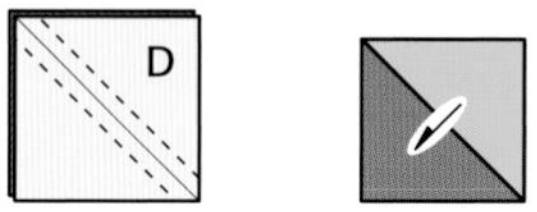

Make 32.

2. Sew a tan D triangle to adjacent sides of 16 triangle squares from step 1 as shown. To the remaining 16 triangle squares, sew a brown E square to one pink end and a tan D triangle to the red end as shown. Make sure the diagonal of each triangle square is positioned as shown.

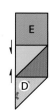

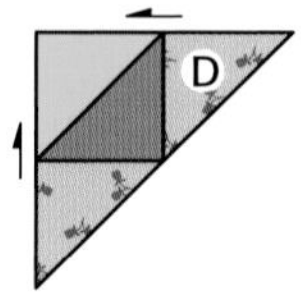

Make 16.

Make 16.

3. Sew the units from step 2 together to make 16 large pieced triangles.

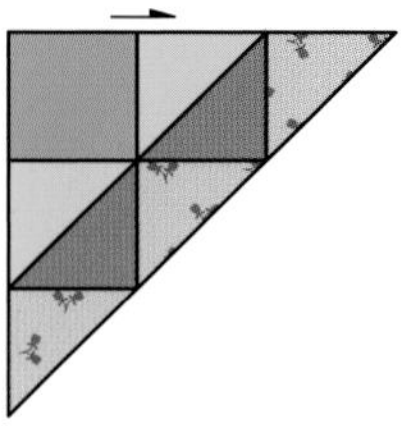

Make 16.

4. Sew large pieced triangles to opposite sides of four cream F squares. Repeat, adding triangles to the remaining sides of the squares to complete four Garden Path Variation blocks.

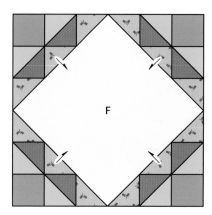

Garden Path Variation Block
Make 4.

5. Repeat step 1, using a cream D square on a red D square. Make four of these to yield eight triangle squares.

6. Repeat steps 2–4 to make one finished block with cream triangles rather than pink triangles.

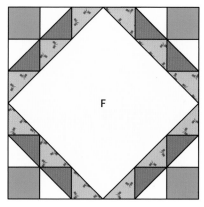

Garden Path Variation Block
Make 1.

ADDING THE APPLIQUÉ

Referring to "Appliqué Techniques" on page 12, use the method of your choice to prepare the appliqué flowers and leaves (patterns on pages 96–100).

Appliqué a different flower cluster on each center square of the Garden Path Variation blocks. Embellish the flower centers with embroidery and a Pigma pen for shading as indicated on the patterns.

Cutting for Borders and Binding					
Fabric	**Piece**	**Number of Strips**	**Strip Width**	**First Cut**	**Second Cut**
Pink	D	1	2⅞"	12 squares, 2⅞" x 2⅞"	Cut all squares ◻
Red	B	1	5¼"	3 squares, 5¼" x 5¼"	Cut all squares ⊠
Brown	E	1	2½"	12 squares, 2½" x 2½"	
Green floral	B	1	5¼"	6 squares, 5¼" x 5¼"	Cut all squares ⊠
	E	1	2½"	16 squares, 2½" x 2½"	
	Outer border	6	5½"		
	Binding	6	2¼"		

MAKING THE PIECED BORDERS

1. Referring to step 3 of "Piecing the Gentleman's Fancy Blocks" on page 92, make 12 units with red and green floral B triangles and pink D triangles. Sew green floral E squares to eight of the units, and brown E squares to the remaining four units.

Make 8.

Make 4.

2. Sew a border section with green end squares to each end of a border section with brown end squares as shown. Make four. Sew a brown E square to opposite ends of two of the borders.

Make 2.

Make 2.

ASSEMBLING THE QUILT TOP

1. Lay out the Gentleman's Fancy blocks and Garden Path Variation blocks in three rows of three blocks each, beginning with a Garden Path Variation block and alternating the blocks as shown in the quilt assembly diagram, opposite.

2. Once you are satisfied with the placement of your appliqué blocks, sew the blocks together in rows and then join the rows.

3. Attach the shorter pieced borders to opposite sides of the quilt top. Add the longer pieced borders to the top and bottom of the quilt top.

4. Referring to "Squared Corners" on page 25, measure the quilt top, piece the 5½"-wide green floral strips together end to end, and from the long strip cut two borders to fit the top and bottom of your quilt. Pin and sew the borders to the quilt, and then measure, trim, pin, and sew side borders to the quilt.

FINISHING THE QUILT

Referring to "Finishing the Quilt" on page 27, prepare the backing fabric and then layer the backing, batting, and quilt top. After basting the layers together, hand or machine quilt as desired and then bind your quilt, using the 2¼"-wide green floral strips.

Quilt Assembly

Appliqué Patterns

Appliqué Patterns

Embroider details as indicated.

········ Stem stitch

Appliqué Patterns

Embroider details as indicated.

 Stem stitch

 Chain stitch

Appliqué Patterns

Appliqué Patterns

Embroider details as indicated.

.... Stem stitch

⬭ Chain stitch

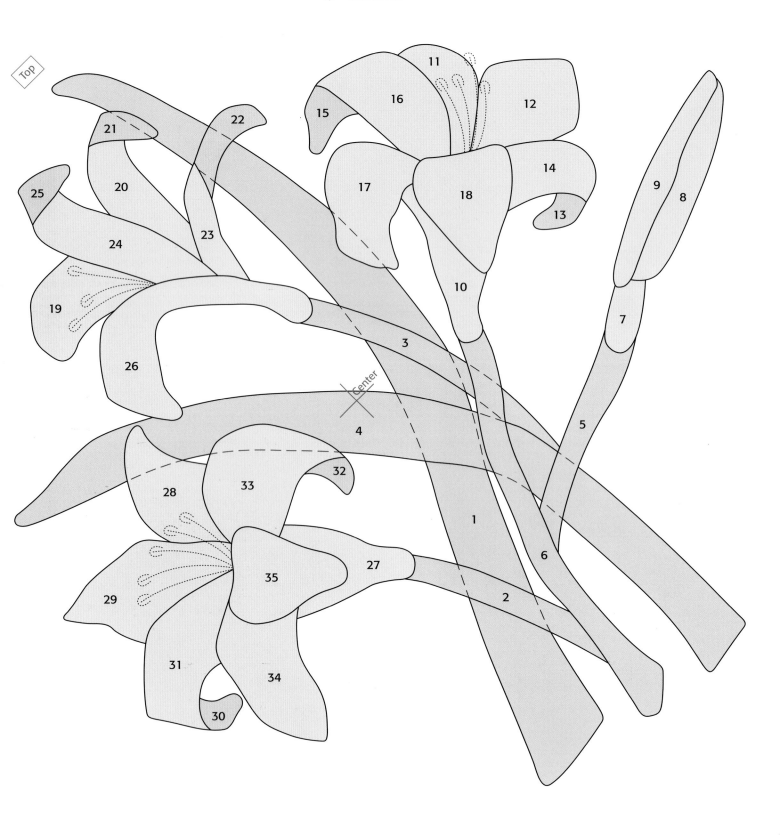

Interlocked Mosaic Stars

*Designed by Claudia Olson; made by Linda Riesterer, 2001, Wenatchee, Washington;
machine quilted by Jill Therriault.*

This intriguing quilt is made with Interlocked Mosaic Arrows and Eccentric Star blocks. Upon first glance, it's hard to see where the various blocks are used because some of the mosaic blocks are modified to allow appliqué in the centers, creating Interlocked Mosaic blocks, while others are completely pieced. Additionally, the Eccentric Star blocks are mirror-image blocks, and by rotating the position of the blocks in the quilt, they create either a light or dark frame around the adjacent appliqué blocks. Finally, the blocks are set on point, and half blocks and quarter blocks are used to complete the design.

Finished Quilt Size: 61" x 61"
Finished Block Size: 12"

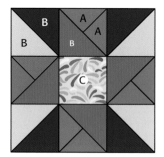

Eccentric Star Block

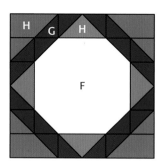

Interlocked Mosaic Block

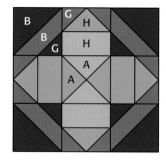

Interlocked Mosaic Arrows Block

MATERIALS

Yardages are based on 42"-wide fabrics.

2⅝ yards of dark purple print for blocks, outer border, and binding

1⅜ yards of navy blue print for blocks

⅝ yard of dark magenta print for star blocks and inner border*

⅝ yard of gray print for star blocks

⅝ yard of white print for appliqué backgrounds

⅜ yard of multicolored print for star blocks

⅜ yard of lavender print for mosaic blocks

⅜ yard of light purple print for mosaic blocks

⅜ yard of teal print for star blocks

⅜ yard of medium purple print for mosaic blocks

¼ yard of medium magenta print for mosaic blocks

Scraps of blues, purples, pinks, maroons, and greens for appliqués

3¾ yards of backing fabric

67" x 67" piece of batting

The yardage given is enough for borders cut across the width of the fabric. If you prefer to cut lengthwise borders, you'll need 1¾ yards of dark magenta print.

			Cutting for Eccentric Star Blocks		
Fabric	**Piece**	**Number of Strips**	**Strip Width**	**First Cut**	**Second Cut**
Dark magenta	A	2	5¼"	9 squares, 5¼" x 5¼"	
Teal	A	2	5¼"	9 squares, 5¼" x 5¼"	
Dark purple	B	3	4⅞"	18 squares, 4⅞" x 4⅞"	Cut all squares ◨
Gray	B	2	4⅞"	12 squares, 4⅞" x 4⅞"	
	D	1	6⅞"	2 squares, 6⅞" x 6⅞"	Cut all squares ⊠
Navy	B	2	4⅞"	12 squares, 4⅞" x 4⅞"	
	D	1	6⅞"	4 squares, 6⅞" x 6⅞"	Cut all squares ⊠
Multicolored	C	1	4½"	4 squares, 4½" x 4½"	
	D	1	6⅞"	2 squares, 6⅞" x 6⅞"	Cut all squares ⊠
	E	Use remainder of 6⅞" strip above	3¾"	2 squares, 3¾" x 3¾"	Cut all squares ◨

PIECING THE ECCENTRIC STAR BLOCKS

You will need four full Eccentric Star blocks, eight half blocks, and four corner blocks for this quilt.

Full Blocks

1. Referring to "Quarter-Square Triangles" on page 23, position a dark magenta A square on a teal A square. Sew to the right side of the drawn lines so that the teal triangles will be on the right side of each triangle pair. Cut and press. Make nine to yield 36 triangle pairs.

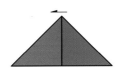

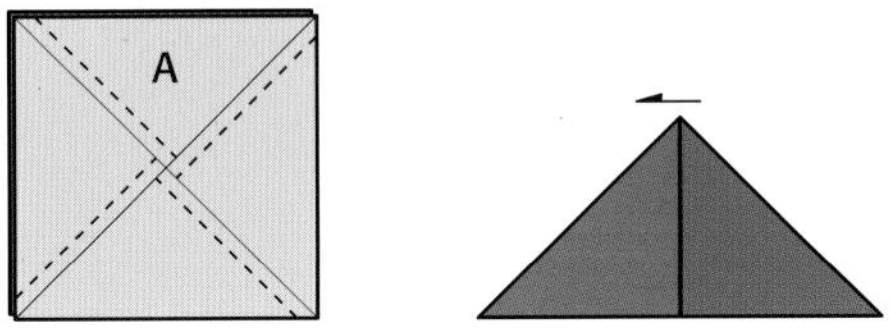

Make 36.

2. Sew the triangle pairs made in step 1 to a dark purple B triangle as shown. Make 36 of these star-point units.

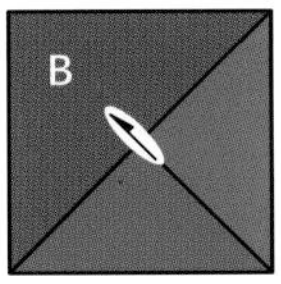

Make 36.

3. Referring to "Half-Square Triangles" on page 23, position a gray B square on a navy B square. Stitch, cut, and press. Make 10 to yield 20 triangle squares.

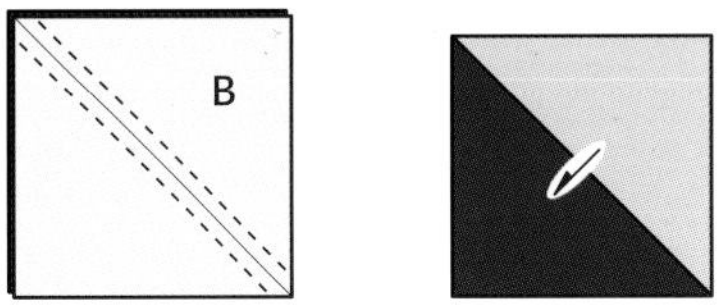

Make 20.

4. Lay out four star-point units from step 2, four triangle squares from step 3, and one multicolored C square as shown, playing close attention to the color positioning for each unit. Sew the units together in rows and then join the rows to complete an Eccentric Star block. Repeat to make a total of four blocks.

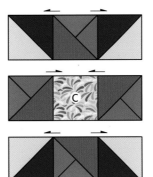

Eccentric Star Block
Make 4.

Mirror-Image Half Blocks

Pay close attention to color placement as you assemble the eight half blocks; you need four with the colors arranged one way and four arranged to create mirror-image units.

1. Using the leftover star-point units from step 2 on page 103, sew a gray D triangle and a multicolored D triangle to the dark purple sides of a star-point unit as shown. Make four.

   To four of the remaining star-point units, sew a gray D triangle and a multicolored D triangle, but notice how the star-point unit is rotated and the placement of the multicolored and gray triangles has been reversed.

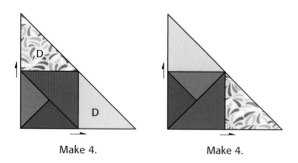

Make 4.   Make 4.

2. Using the navy/gray triangle squares from step 3 above, sew them to star-point units as shown. Make four of each combination. Attach a navy D triangle to the opposite side of the star-point units as shown.

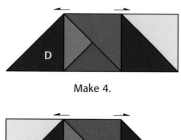

Make 4.

Make 4.

3. Sew the units from step 1 to those from step 2, taking care to match the color combinations correctly. Make four of each to complete the eight half blocks, four of each combination.

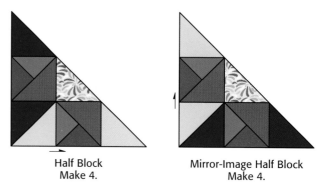

Half Block
Make 4.

Mirror-Image Half Block
Make 4.

Corner Blocks

Using the remaining four star-point units, sew navy D triangles to opposite sides as shown, paying careful attention to color placement. Attach a multicolored E triangle to each unit to complete four corner blocks.

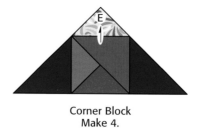

Corner Block
Make 4.

				Cutting for Interlocked Mosaic and Interlocked Mosaic Arrows Blocks		

Fabric	Piece	Number of Strips	Strip Width	First Cut
Navy	B	1	4⅞"	8 squares, 4⅞" x 4⅞"
	G	6	2½"	96 squares, 2½" x 2½"
	I	2	2⅞"	10 squares, 2⅞" x 2⅞"
White	F	2	8½"	5 squares, 8½" x 8½"
Medium purple	H	2	4½"	20 rectangles, 2½" x 4½"
Dark purple	B	1	4⅞"	8 squares, 4⅞" x 4⅞"
	G	2	2½"	32 squares, 2½" x 2½"
	H	2	4½"	20 rectangles, 2½" x 4½"
	I	2	2⅞"	10 squares, 2⅞" x 2⅞"
Light purple	A	1	5¼"	2 squares, 5¼" x 5¼"
	H	1	4½"	8 rectangles, 2½" x 4½"
Lavender	A	1	5¼"	2 squares, 5¼" x 5¼"
	H	1	4½"	8 rectangles, 2½" x 4½"
Medium magenta	H	1	4½"	16 rectangles, 2½" x 4½"

PIECING THE INTERLOCKED MOSAIC BLOCKS

This quilt uses five Interlocked Mosaic blocks with appliqué centers and four Interlocked Mosaic Arrows blocks.

Interlocked Mosaic Blocks with Appliqué Centers

1. Referring to "Quick Corner Triangles" on page 24, position a navy G square on the corner of a white F square. Stitch to make the triangle corner. Press. Repeat, stitching a navy square to each corner. Make five.

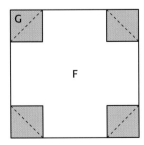

Make 5.

2. Using the technique for quick corner triangles, sew a navy G square to one corner of a medium purple H rectangle. Repeat on the opposite corner to make a flying-geese unit. Make 20.

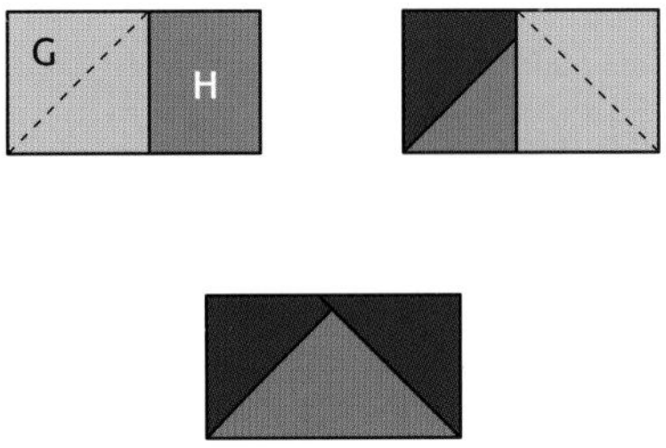

Make 20.

3. In the same manner, sew a navy G square to one end of a dark purple H rectangle. Make 10 with the triangle on one end and 10 with the triangle on the opposite end as shown.

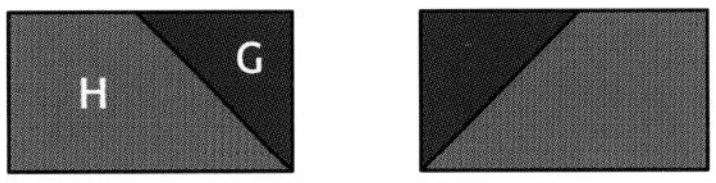

Make 10 each.

4. Referring to "Half-Square Triangles," position a navy I square on a dark purple I square. Stitch, cut, and press. Make 10 to yield 20 triangle squares. Sew one of these triangle squares to either side of 10 of the flying-geese units from step 2 as shown.

Make 20.

Make 10.

5. Lay out the various units for one block as shown. Sew the units together in rows and then join the rows to complete one block. Repeat to make five Interlocked Mosaic blocks.

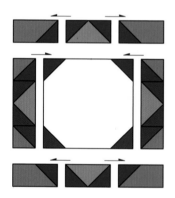 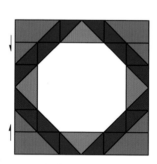

Interlocked Mosaic Block
Make 5.

6. Referring to "Appliqué Techniques" on page 12, use the method of your choice to prepare the floral appliqués (patterns on pages 109–111). Appliqué one design on each block. Embroider stamens and flower centers according to the placement indicated on the individual flower patterns.

Interlocked Mosaic Arrows Blocks

1. Using the technique for half-square triangles, position a navy B square on a dark purple B square. Stitch, cut, and press. Make eight to yield 16 triangle squares.

Make 16.

2. Using the technique for quick corner triangles on page 24, position a navy G square on the dark purple corner of each triangle square from step 1. Sew, trim, and press. Make 16.

Make 16.

3. Referring to "Quarter-Square Triangles" on page 23, position a light purple A square on a lavender A square. Sew to the right side of the drawn lines so that the lavender triangles will be on the right side of each triangle pair. Cut and press. Make two to yield eight triangle pairs. Join the triangle pairs as shown to make four pieced squares.

 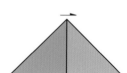

Make 4.

4. Using the technique for quick corner triangles, stitch a dark purple G square to a medium magenta H rectangle. Repeat on the other end of the rectangle to make a flying-geese unit. Make 16.

Make 16.

5. Sew a light purple H rectangle to the bottom of half of the flying-geese units and a lavender H rectangle to the bottom of the remaining flying-geese units.

Make 8 each.

6. Lay out the various block units as shown, paying careful attention to color placement. Sew the units together in rows and then join the rows. Repeat to make a total of four Interlocked Mosaic Arrows blocks.

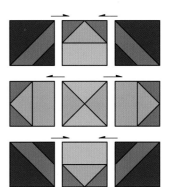

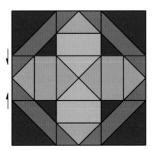

Interlocked Mosaic Arrows Block
Make 4.

Cutting for Borders and Binding			
Fabric	**Piece**	**Number of Strips**	**Strip Width**
Dark magenta	Inner border	6	1½"
Dark purple	Outer border	7	4¼"
	Binding	7	2¼"

ASSEMBLING THE QUILT TOP

1. Referring to the quilt assembly diagram, lay out the quilt blocks, half blocks, and corner blocks in diagonal rows, alternating the blocks as shown. Make sure all of the appliqué blocks are facing in the same direction. Be careful when placing the Eccentric Star half blocks because the blocks are sometimes rotated to move the positioning of the gray and navy triangles.

2. After reviewing the layout to make sure everything is positioned correctly, sew the blocks together in rows and then join the rows.

3. Sew the 1½"-wide dark magenta border strips together end to end. From this long strip cut four 58"-long border strips. In the same manner, sew

the 4¼"-wide dark purple border strips together end to end and from the long strip cut four 65"-long border strips. Matching midpoints, sew each dark magenta strip to a dark purple strip.

4. Referring to "Mitered Corners" on page 25, attach the borders with the narrow dark magenta strips toward the quilt center. Miter the corners to complete the quilt top.

FINISHING THE QUILT

Referring to "Finishing the Quilt" on page 27, prepare the backing fabric and then layer the backing, batting, and quilt top. After basting the layers together, hand or machine quilt as desired and then bind your quilt using the 2¼"-wide dark purple strips.

Quilt Assembly

Appliqué Patterns

Enlarge patterns 133%.

Appliqué Patterns

Enlarge patterns 133%.
Embroider details as indicated.

⚬   French knot

········   Stem stitch

No Squirrels Allowed

Designed, made, and hand quilted by Claudia Olson, 2000, Wenatchee, Washington.

Three chickadees and a squirrel are nestled on tree branches and set among Arrow Points and Patchwork Pinwheels blocks in this autumn-toned quilt. I pieced the blocks in progressively darker shadings and set them with the lightest blocks in the center of the quilt and the darkest ones at the outer edges. To allow for the appliqué, I replaced complex piecing in some places with simpler background fabric shapes. Notice how the appliqué designs extend beyond block boundaries, and branch beginnings are tucked in seams or behind leaves.

Finished Quilt Size: 66½" x 66½"
Finished Block Size: 12"

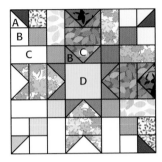 

Arrow Points Block   Patchwork Pinwheels Block

MATERIALS

Yardages are based on 42"-wide fabrics.

1⅝ yards of black floral print for blocks and border

1⅜ yards of dark fall print for blocks, borders, and binding

1 yard of cream print for appliqué background

⅞ yard of medium fall print for blocks and border

¾ yard of dark wine print for blocks and border

⅝ yard total of assorted medium beige prints for blocks and border

⅝ yard of dark green print for blocks and border

⅝ yard of light fall print for blocks

½ yard of dark beige print for blocks and border

½ yard of medium brown print for branches and acorns

⅜ yard of light beige print for blocks

⅜ yard of green small-scale leaf print for blocks

⅜ yard of light green print for blocks

⅜ yard of dark gold print for blocks and border

¼ yard of gold leaf print for blocks

¼ yard total or scraps of assorted medium green prints for blocks

¼ yard of medium wine print for blocks

⅛ yard of light gold print for blocks

⅛ yard of medium gold print for blocks

¼ yard of dark brown print for acorn appliqués

⅛ yard of light wine print for blocks

Assorted scraps of beige, black, brown, dark red or rust, gray, green, gold, wine, and white prints for appliqués

4 yards of backing fabric

72" x 72" piece of batting

Black, brown, dark gray, and white embroidery flosses

Brown Pigma pen

Cutting for Arrow Points Blocks

Fabric	Piece	Number of Strips	Strip Width	First Cut
Cream	A	1	2⅜"	8 squares, 2⅜" x 2⅜"
	B	2	2"	32 squares, 2" x 2"
	C	2	3½"	40 rectangles, 2" x 3½"
	D	1	3½"	4 squares, 3½" x 3½"
	E	Use remainder of 3½" strip above	3½"	4 rectangles, 3½" x 6½"
Light beige	A	1	2⅜"	4 squares, 2⅜" x 2⅜"
	B	1	2"	16 squares, 2" x 2"
Medium beiges	B	1	2"	8 squares, 2" x 2"
	C	1	3½"	8 rectangles, 2" x 3½"
Dark beige	C	1	3½"	4 rectangles, 2" x 3½"
Green leaf print	A	1	2⅜"	4 squares, 2⅜" x 2⅜"
	B	1	2"	16 squares, 2" x 2"
Gold leaf print	C	1	3½"	16 rectangles, 2" x 3½"
Light green	A	1	2⅜"	4 squares, 2⅜" x 2⅜"
	B	1	2"	8 squares, 2" x 2"
Medium greens	B	3	2"	56 squares, 2" x 2"
Dark green	A	1	2⅜"	12 squares, 2⅜" x 2⅜"
	B	2	2"	40 squares, 2" x 2"
Light wine	B	1	2"	16 squares, 2" x 2"
Medium wine	B	2	2"	32 squares, 2" x 2"
Dark wine	B	4	2"	28 squares, 2" x 2" (leave 2 strips uncut)
Light gold	D	1	3½"	1 square, 3½" x 3½"
Medium gold	D	1	3½"	4 squares, 3½" x 3½"
Dark gold	D	1	3½"	8 squares, 3½" x 3½"
Light fall print	B	1	2"	16 squares, 2" x 2"
	C	3	3½"	36 rectangles, 2" x 3½"
Medium fall print	B	2	2"	32 squares, 2" x 2"
	C	4	3½"	44 rectangles, 2" x 3½"
Dark fall print	B	2	2"	32 squares, 2" x 2"
	C	2	3½"	32 rectangles, 2" x 3½"
Black floral	B	1	2"	20 squares, 2" x 2"
	C	4	3½"	56 rectangles, 2" x 3½"

PIECING THE ARROW POINTS BLOCKS

This quilt uses 13 Arrow Points blocks; however, they are not identical when it comes to color placement.

Four of the blocks are medium-toned, four are dark, four are a combination of part medium and part light, and one is light. The instructions begin with piecing the medium blocks, and then abbreviated directions follow for making the blocks in other colorways.

While the blocks are complex, each one can be broken down into easy-to-piece units for the corners, center, and arrows (sides) of the block. The fabric key will help you keep track of the similar colors as you work on the different color combinations.

Fabric Key

Cream	Light wine
Light beige	Medium wine
Medium beige	Dark wine
Dark beige	Light gold
Green small-scale leaf print	Medium gold
Gold leaf print	Dark gold
Light green	Light fall print
Medium green	Medium fall print
Dark green	Dark fall print
	Black floral

Medium Arrow Points Blocks

1. Referring to "Half-Square Triangles" on page 23, position a cream A square on a light green A square. Stitch, cut, and press. Repeat with A square combinations of cream and dark green, green leaf and dark green, and light beige and dark green as shown. Make two of each color combination to yield four triangle squares of each.

Make 4 each.

2. Using cream, light beige, and green leaf print B squares and light, medium, and dark wine B squares and triangle squares from step 1, lay out the pieces for four-patch units as shown. Make sure each triangle square is oriented correctly before stitching the four-patch units together. Make four of each color combination.

Make 4 each.

3. Using additional light, medium, and dark wine B squares and cream, light fall print, and gold leaf print C rectangles with the four patches from step 2, lay out the pieces for the block corner units as shown. Sew the pieces together in rows and then join the rows to complete a corner unit. Make four of each color combination as shown.

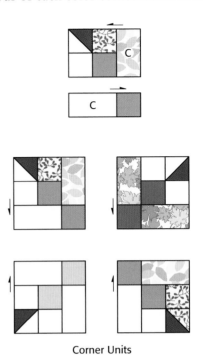

Corner Units
Make 4 each.

4. Referring to "Quick Corner Triangles" on page 24, sew a medium green B square on a medium fall print C rectangle. Repeat, sewing a medium green square on the other end to make a flying-geese unit. Make eight. In the same manner, sew medium fall print squares on a black floral rectangle, light fall print squares on a cream rectangle, and medium green squares on a light fall print rectangle. Make eight flying-geese units of each color combination.

Make 8.

Make 8 each.

5. Sew the flying-geese units from step 4 on opposite sides of a medium fall or a light fall print C rectangle, matching colors. Make eight of each of the arrow units as shown.

Arrow Units
Make 8 each.

6. Lay out the corner units and arrow units as shown with a medium gold D square in the center to form one block. Sew the units together in rows and then join the rows. Repeat to make four matching blocks.

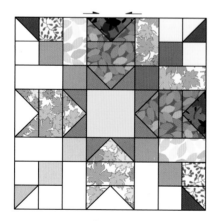

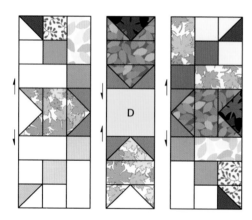

Medium Block
Make 4.

Dark Arrow Points Blocks

These blocks are made in the same way as the medium Arrow Points blocks. Only the colors have changed, and rectangles have replaced triangles in three of the corners. Paying careful attention to the color and letter name of each piece, make the corner units and arrow units, and combine them with dark gold D squares to make four dark Arrow Points blocks.

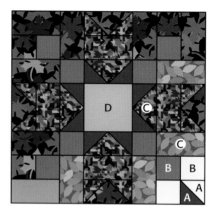

Dark Block
Make 4.

For each block, you will need the following pieces:

For corner units

1 light beige A square (yields triangle squares for 2 blocks)

1 dark green A squares (yields triangle squares for 2 blocks)

2 light beige B squares

8 dark wine B squares

3 black floral B squares

4 medium fall print C rectangles

6 black floral C rectangles

1 dark beige C rectangle

For arrow units

8 dark green B squares

8 dark fall print B squares

8 dark fall print C rectangles

4 black floral C rectangles

For center unit

1 dark gold D square

Light Arrow Points Block

Only one of these blocks is needed for the center of the quilt. The assembly is different from the other Arrow Points blocks because the arrow points have been replaced by cream fabric to allow space for appliqué.

1. Referring to "Half-Square Triangles" on page 23, position a cream A square on a light green A square. Stitch, cut, and press. Make two to yield four triangle squares.

2. Lay out a triangle square, two cream B squares, and one light wine B square as shown. Sew the pieces together in rows and then join the rows. Repeat to make a total of four corner units.

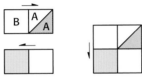

Make 4.

3. Using the technique for quick corner triangles, sew a light green B square to each end of a cream C rectangle to make a flying-geese unit. Repeat to make four units.

Make 4.

4. Lay out the four flying-geese units, four light wine B squares, and one light gold D square as shown. Sew the pieces together in rows and then join the rows to complete the star center of the block.

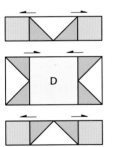 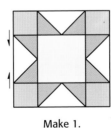

Make 1.

5. Lay out the star center, the four corner units from step 2, and the four cream E rectangles as shown. Sew the pieces together in rows and then join the rows to complete one light Arrow Points block.

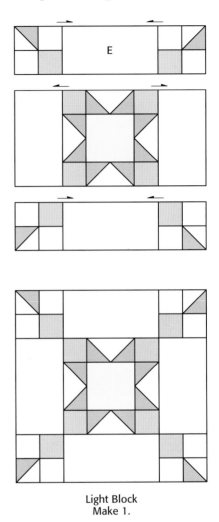

Light Block
Make 1.

Combination Arrow Points Blocks

These blocks are made in the same way as the medium Arrow Points blocks. However, some of the colors have changed and one of the arrow points has been replaced by a plain cream square. Paying careful attention to the color and letter name of each piece, make the corner units and arrow units, and combine them with dark gold D squares to make four combination Arrow Points blocks. Note that while there are only two color combinations for the corner units, they are pieced as mirror images, so each corner is unique.

Note: A branch end will be inserted between the squares sewn in the corner unit of two combination Arrow Points blocks. Please see the appliqué patterns for placement.

Combination Block
Make 4.

For each combination block, you will need the following pieces:

For corner units

1 medium green B square

1 cream A square

2 cream B squares

2 green leaf print B squares

4 medium wine B squares

4 dark wine B squares

2 medium beige B squares

2 gold leaf print C rectangles

2 medium fall print C rectangles

2 cream C rectangles

2 medium beige C rectangles

For arrow points

8 medium green B squares

4 medium fall print B squares

2 black floral B squares

4 medium fall print C rectangles

4 black floral C rectangles

1 light fall print C rectangle

1 cream C rectangle

1 cream D square

For center unit

1 dark gold D square

Cutting for 8 Patchwork Pinwheels and 4 Plain Blocks					
Fabric	**Piece**	**Number of Strips**	**Strip Width**	**First Cut**	**Second Cut**
Cream	F	1	12½"	4 squares, 12½" x 12½"	
Light beige	A	2	2⅜"	20 squares, 2⅜" x 2⅜"	
	B	1	2"	16 squares, 2" x 2"	
Medium beiges	B	1	2"	16 squares, 2" x 2"	
	C	1	2"	8 rectangles, 2" x 3½"	
Dark beige	B	1	2"	16 squares, 2" x 2"	
	C	1	2"	8 rectangles, 2" x 3½"	
Green leaf print	A	1	2⅜"	4 squares, 2⅜" x 2⅜"	
	B	1	2"	16 squares, 2" x 2"	
Gold leaf print	B	1	2"	16 squares, 2" x 2"	
Light green	A	1	2⅜"	4 squares, 2⅜" x 2⅜"	Cut all squares ◻
Dark green	A	2	2⅜"	28 squares, 2⅜" x 2⅜"	Cut 4 squares ◻
Dark wine	B	4	2"	64 squares, 2" x 2"	
Light fall print	B	1	2"	16 squares, 2" x 2"	
	C	2	3½"	32 rectangles, 2" x 3½"	
Medium fall print	B	1	2"	16 squares, 2" x 2"	
Black floral	F	3	6½"	32 rectangles, 3½" x 6½"	

PIECING THE PATCHWORK PINWHEELS BLOCKS

1. Referring to steps 1 and 2 of "Medium Arrow Points Blocks" on page 115, make four dark green/green leaf print triangle squares and four dark green/light beige triangle squares. Lay out these triangle squares with green leaf print, dark wine, and light beige B squares as shown. Sew the units together to make eight of each corner unit.

Make 8 each.

2. Make the other two corner units as shown. One unit requires a dark wine B square, a medium beige B square, and a medium beige C rectangle. The other uses a dark wine B square and dark beige B and C pieces. Make eight of each.

Make 8 each.

3. Using the technique for quick corner triangles, position a gold leaf print B square on the top left corner of a black floral F rectangle. Stitch, cut, and press. Repeat, sewing a light fall print B square to the top right corner of the rectangle as shown. Make eight. In the same manner, make eight mirror-image black floral rectangles with the gold leaf print on the right and the light fall print on the left.

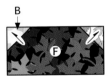 

Make 8 each.

4. In the same manner as step 3, sew four black floral F rectangles with dark beige B squares on the top left corner and medium beige B squares on the top right corner as shown. In the same manner, make four mirror-image black floral rectangles with dark beige B squares on the right and medium beige B squares on the left corner. Make eight more black floral rectangles with medium fall print squares on both corners.

Make 4 each.

Make 8.

5. Using the technique for half-square triangles, position a light beige A square on a dark green A square. Stitch, cut, and press. Make 16 to yield 32 triangle squares. Join the triangle squares together to make eight pinwheels as shown.

Make 8.

6. Lay out a pinwheel, four light fall print C rectangles, and four dark wine B squares as shown. Sew the units together in rows and then join the rows to complete the block center. Make eight.

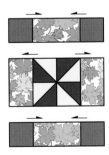 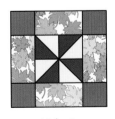

Make 8.

7. Lay out the corner units, the black floral rectangles, and the pinwheel centers as shown. Note that block B (on the bottom) is somewhat of a mirror image of block A (on top). Make four of each, paying careful attention to the color placement of each unit.

Patchwork Pinwheels Block A
Make 4.

Patchwork Pinwheels Block B
Make 4.

ADDING THE APPLIQUÉ

1. For the plain blocks, appliqué the inside edges of two light green and two dark green A triangles to the corners of the cream F squares, positioning the triangles as shown. The triangles will form pinwheels when the blocks are set side by side with the pieced blocks.

2. Referring to "Appliqué Techniques" on page 12, use the method of your choice to prepare the appliqué leaves, squirrel, birds, and acorns (patterns on pages 124 and 125). For the leaves, use the green, gold, wine, and brown fabrics to make the following number of leaves: leaf 1 (2), leaf 2 (1), leaf 3 (8), leaf 4 (1), leaf 5 (3), leaf 6 (5), leaf 7 (9), leaf 8 (1), leaf 9 (1), leaf 10 (2), leaf 11 (1). Make one each of the three birds, using black, white, and gray fabrics. Make one squirrel from brown fabric. For the branches, use medium brown fabric and cut seven bias strips 1⅛" wide.

3. Appliqué shapes as follows, referring to the "Appliqué Placement Guides" on page 126. Notice that some leaves will overlap other blocks and should be left until the blocks are joined together.
   - Appliqué branches to the cream backgrounds first. The thickest ends of the long branches are ½" wide and they narrow to ¼". Notice that smaller branches are tucked under longer branches. Leave free the ends of branches that will be sewn into the seam allowance between blocks when the quilt is assembled. Notice also that one bird is behind a branch, which will need to be left loose for now.
   - Appliqué leaves and acorns to branches.
   - Appliqué birds and squirrels in the order shown by piece numbers.

4. Embroider acorn stems using a chain stitch and two strands of brown embroidery floss. Embroider bird legs and feet using a chain stitch and two strands of dark gray floss. Embroider the underside of the squirrel's stomach using two strands of brown floss. Embroider the squirrel's eye, birds' eyes, and birds' beaks using a satin stitch and two strands of black floss. Make a white spot in each eye by embroidering two small satin stitches with two strands of white floss.

5. Shade the squirrel's ear using a brown Pigma pen.

Cutting for Borders and Binding

Fabric	Piece	Number of Strips	Strip Width	First Cut
Medium beiges	A	1	2⅜"	12 squares, 2⅜" x 2⅜"
	B	3	2"	64 squares, 2" x 2"
Dark beige	A	1	2⅜"	12 squares, 2⅜" x 2⅜"
	B	2	2"	40 squares, 2" x 2"
Dark green	A	2	2⅜"	20 squares, 2⅜" x 2⅜"
	B	Use remainder of 2⅜" strip above	2"	4 squares, 2" x 2"
Dark wine	A	2	2⅜"	20 squares, 2⅜" x 2⅜"
Dark gold	A	2	2⅜"	20 squares, 2⅜" x 2⅜"
	B	Use remainder of 2⅜" strip above	2"	4 squares, 2" x 2"
Medium fall print	A	1	2⅜"	12 squares, 2⅜" x 2⅜"
	B	2	2"	24 squares, 2" x 2"
Dark fall print	A	1	2⅜"	12 squares, 2⅜" x 2⅜"
	D	3	3½"	32 squares, 3½" x 3½"
	B	1	2"	16 squares, 2" x 2"
	Binding	7	2¼"	
Black floral	A	2	2⅜"	20 squares, 2⅜" x 2⅜"
	C	1	2"	8 rectangles, 2" x 3½"
	B	3	2"	56 squares, 2" x 2"

MAKING THE PIECED BORDER

1. Using the technique for quick corner triangles, position a black floral B square on each corner of a dark fall print D square. Stitch, cut, and press to make a square-in-a-square unit. Make eight, two for each border. In the same manner, make eight units with medium beige corners, and four with medium fall print corners. Label these units as "unit 1."

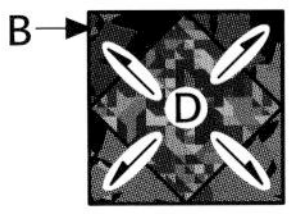

Unit 1
Make 8.

Unit 1
Make 8.

Unit 1
Make 4.

2. Repeat step 1 to make four units with two dark beige opposite corners, one dark green corner, and one dark gold corner. In the same manner, make eight units with two medium beige adjacent corners and two black floral corners as shown. Label the units with a green and a gold corner as "corner units." Label the other units "unit 1."

Corner Unit
Make 4.

Unit 1
Make 4.

3. Using the half-square-triangle technique, position a dark gold A square on a black floral A square. Stitch, cut, and press. Repeat with any other A squares of your choice, using dark green, dark fall print, dark wine, black floral, dark gold, dark beige, or medium beige squares. Make a total of 64 to yield 128 triangle squares.

4. Sew three triangle squares together with one B square to make a broken pinwheel as shown. Make eight with dark beige backgrounds, eight with medium beige backgrounds, eight with black floral backgrounds, and eight that are mixed. Label these units "unit 2."

Unit 2
Make 8 each.

5. Using the technique for quick-corner triangles, sew a dark beige B square on one corner of a black floral C rectangle. Repeat, sewing a medium beige B square on the opposite corner. Make a total of four and then make four more with the beige corners reversed.

Make 4 each.

6. Sew medium beige and dark beige B squares together in pairs. Make eight pairs. Sew these to the bottom of the flying-geese units from step 5 so that the beige corners and squares below are matching.

Make 4 each.

7. Sew a pinwheel from step 4 to either side of the pieces from step 6, matching background color as shown. Make four of each. Label these units "unit 3."

Unit 3
Make 4.

Unit 3
Make 4.

8. Sew four triangle squares from step 3 with dark backgrounds together with two dark fall print B squares as shown. Make eight. Label these "unit 4."

Unit 4
Make 8.

9. Sew the units together in the order shown in the diagram. Repeat to make a total of four borders. Attach the corner units from step 2 to the ends of two of the borders.

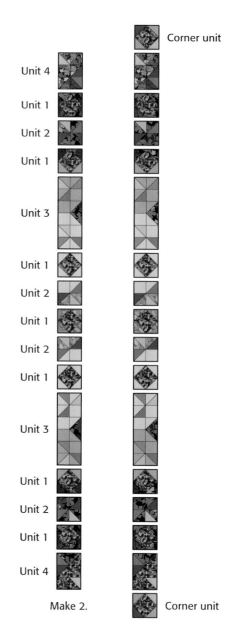

ASSEMBLING THE QUILT TOP

1. Referring to the quilt assembly diagram below, lay out the dark, medium, light, and combination Arrow Points blocks, the Patchwork Pinwheels blocks, and the appliqué blocks. Pay careful attention to keep the dark colors facing toward the outer corners of the quilt.
2. Sew the blocks together in rows and then join the rows.
3. Complete any appliqué where shapes overlap the edges of the blocks. Unpick a few stitches in blocks where branches need to be tucked in. Close seams with machine or hand stitches.
4. Sew a pieced border to each side of the quilt top. Then sew the pieced borders with the corner units to the top and bottom of the quilt.

FINISHING THE QUILT

Referring to "Finishing the Quilt" on page 27, prepare the backing fabric and then layer the backing, batting, and quilt top. After basting the layers together, hand or machine quilt as desired and then bind your quilt, using the 2¼"-wide dark fall print strips.

Quilt Assembly

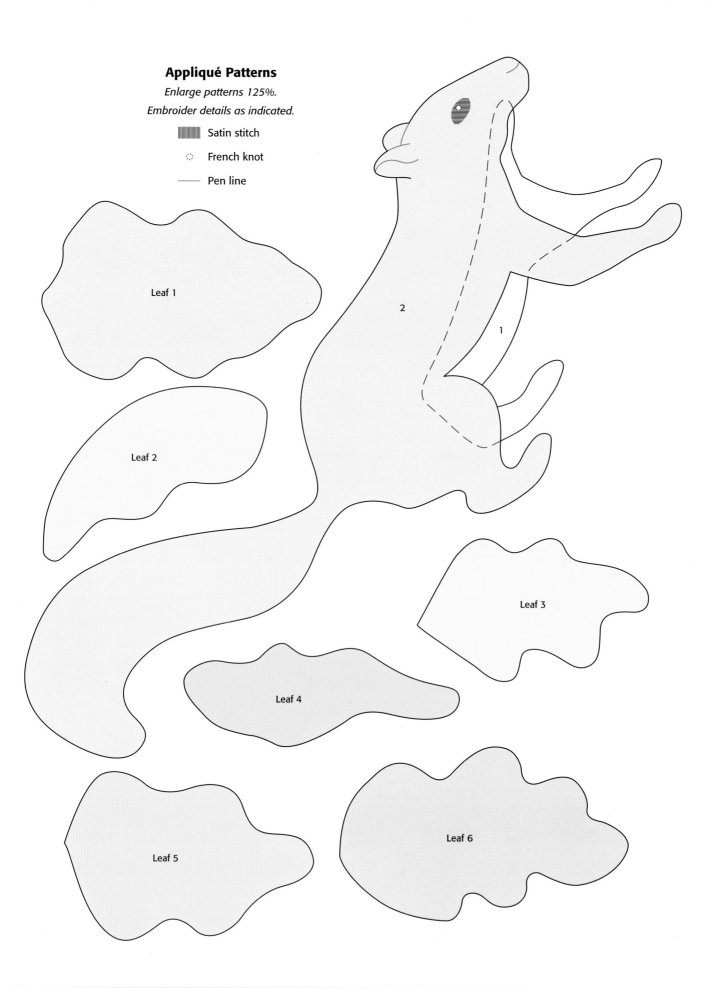

Appliqué Patterns

Enlarge patterns 125%.

Embroider details as indicated.

▥ Satin stitch

⊙ French knot

— Pen line

Leaf 1

Leaf 2

Leaf 3

Leaf 4

Leaf 5

Leaf 6

2

1

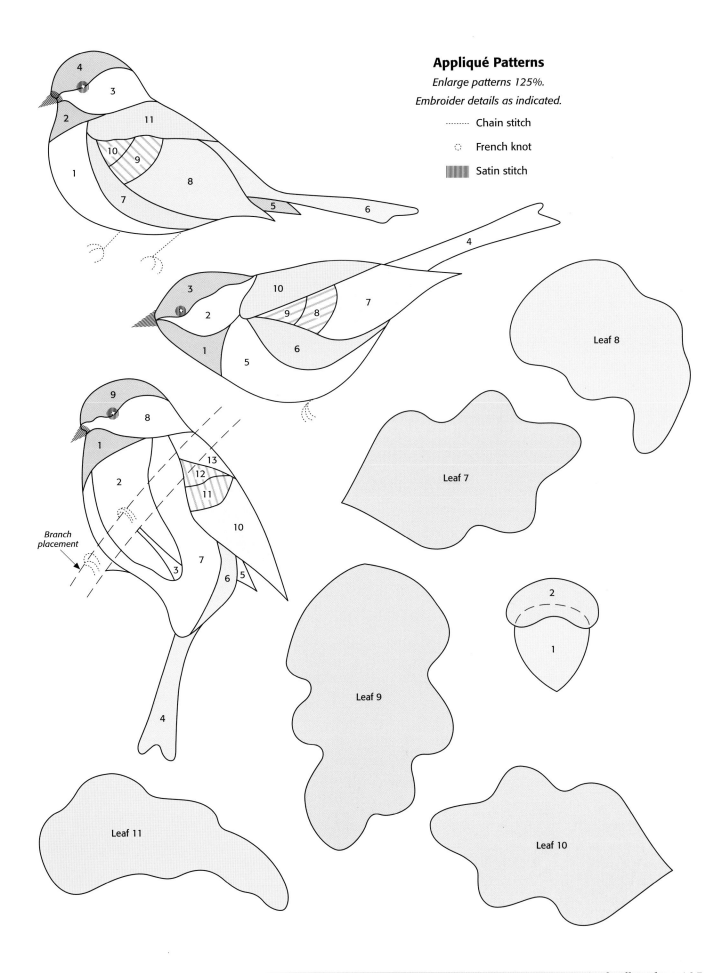

Appliqué Patterns

Enlarge patterns 125%.
Embroider details as indicated.

- ········ Chain stitch
- ⊙ French knot
- ▨ Satin stitch

Appliqué Placement Guides

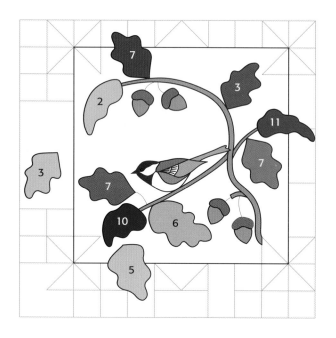

Meet the Author

I was born in California in the days when the land was covered with more fruit trees than houses. I spent equal amounts of time in northern and Southern California, but most of my memories are of Anaheim, where I worked at Disneyland and spent lots of time on the beaches, in the desert, and in the mountains. I graduated from California State University at Fullerton with a bachelor's degree in geography and an elementary teaching degree. I love being with and teaching children.

I moved to Alaska, where I met my husband. We have two college-aged children and now live in Wenatchee, Washington.

I learned to hand sew with my grandmother, Isabel Vincent, at my side. Later, at the age of 12, I learned to machine sew and made most of my school clothes after that. I learned quilting 18 years ago under the instruction of Marsha McCloskey, who inspired me to make two-block quilts. I was never content to leave a quilt in its simplest form, but always looked for ideas to make it more interesting. Finding new ways to set a quilt fascinated me. I soon began teaching quilting classes and found that I enjoyed the role of encouraging new quilters. I began designing quilts and creating patterns in 1998. With the help of more than 20 good quilting friends, I wrote my first quilting book in 2001. I have since appeared on the television program *Simply Quilts* with hostess Alex Anderson, and have had a quilt featured in *Quiltmaker* magazine.

Acknowledgments

I would like to extend gratitude to my kind quilting friends who offered to make quilts for this project. Without their generous help, this book would not have been possible. Thank you Doni Palmgren, Pat Peyton, Sandy Ashbrook, LaVanche Rhodes, Pam James, Mary Rozendaal, Terry Vaughan, Linda Riesterer, and Karen Sinn.

I would also like to recognize the fine work of my photographer, Brent Kane. He was always able to make the most difficult shots turn out well. I am also grateful to Laurel Strand for her wonderful illustrations and keen eye for color.

Thanks again to my husband and children for their help and support during the writing process. They were always ready to encourage and help me along in my endeavors.

Special recognition goes out to my friends who lent special skills to the processes involved in making these quilts. They helped me understand their unique ways of appliqué and embellishment. They are Sandy Ashbrook, Terry Vaughan, and LaVanche Rhodes. Thanks also to Jill Therriault, who beautifully and creatively machine quilted many of our quilts. She always found time to fit another quilt into her schedule.

Lastly, I would like to thank my editors, Karen Soltys and Liz McGehee, and my publisher for their hard work on this project. You are the ones who help make dreams come true. Thank you for believing in me and seeing my vision.

The Laubach Way to
CURSIVE WRITING

by Kay Koschnick

ISBN 0-88336-909-5

© 1983
New Readers Press
Publishing Division of Laubach Literacy International
Box 131, Syracuse, New York 13210

Printed in the United States of America

Edited by Caroline Blakely
Cover designed by Chris Steenwerth
Lettering by Alice Newman

20   19   18 17   16   15   14

Lesson 1

e i u t

These letters begin with an under-curve like this:

---

e

e

e

e

---

i

i

i

i

---

u

u

u

u

---

t

t

t

t

Practice: Copy the letters.

e e e e e ee ee ee ee ee ee

i i i i i ei ei ei ie ie ie

u u u u u ue ue ue ue ue

t t t t t et ut it te tu ti

Copy the words.

it it it tie tie tie

j p

These letters begin like this:

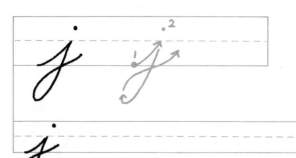

Practice: Copy the words.

jet jet jet jet jet jet jet

pet put pup up pup put

s r

These letters begin with an under-curve like this:

s

s

r

r

Practice: Copy the words.

see sit is us jets pets test

rest rest rest tree sister street

Homework: Copy the words.

up pup pups pet pets jet jets

it sit sits test tests rest rests

see sees tree trees street streets

is us just tie ties tries retire

Write these words: *just test sister tree street puts*

Homework: Copy these phrases.

tie it up   put it up   sit up

just us   just sits   sees us

sister's pup   tries it   sees trees

pup sees it   sister rests

Write these phrases: *pup sits up   sister's street*

Lesson 2

These letters begin with an over-curve like this: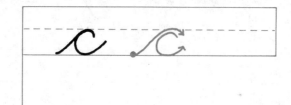

c
c

c

a
a

a

d
d

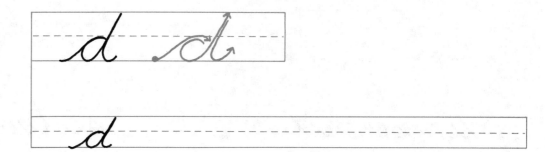

d

Practice: Copy the words.

cup cut ice price picture

at cat ate are car air as

dad did ad sad add dead dear

pat rat jar card care said side

Write these words: *cut car ate are did said*

These letters begin like the letter a: *a* They end with a bottom loop.

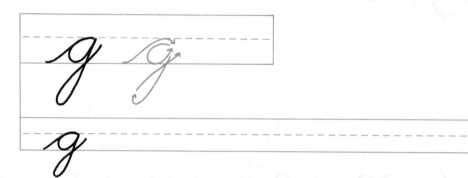

Practice: Copy the words.

gate get gets grass rug egg

quart quarter quarters quit quits

Homework: Copy the words.

cup air care part paper state

address speed stairs repairs did

die died cried tied dried tried

get quarter grass quit gate rug

Write these words: *address part state speed repair*

Homework: Copy these phrases.

a red dress   ate eggs   at a race

cuts paper   passed a car   iced tea

reads ads   gets tired   past us

paid a quarter   are retired

Write these phrases: *car parts   quit it   a pet cat*

Homework: Copy these phrases.

dear dad   add a quart

eat eggs   get a ride   cut prices

a sad picture   as tired as dad

quits cigarettes   gets a quart

Write these phrases: *a quart jar   passed a test*

Lesson 3

These letters begin with a curve like this:

Practice: Copy the words.

in an can pan need nine ten

me meat map made came time

an am man men name menu

six sex tax next taxes sixteen

Write these words: *in time six men name next*

Y Z

These letters begin with a curve like this: ⟋ They end with a bottom loop.

Y

Y Y

Y

Z
Z

Z Z

Z

Practice: Copy the words.

yes yet my may any many

zip zips zipper citizen citizens

Homework: Copy these phrases.

spent ten cents   studying music

next time   didn't eat any meat

must pay my rent   in my arms

a pretty garden   zipped up my tent

Write these phrases: *my name   six men   zip up*

Homework: Copy these phrases.

sun and sand   rain and mud

at camp   cut taxes next year

standing up   started crying again

green eyes   an angry citizen

Write these phrases: *runs and jumps   says yes*

Homework: Copy these phrases.

carrying a gun   a married man

signed my name   dinner at six

can sing   need a gray zipper

painted my apartment yesterday

Write this phrase: *many teenagers under sixteen*

Lesson 4

These letters begin with a tall loop like this:

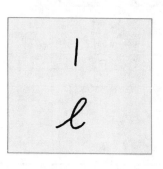

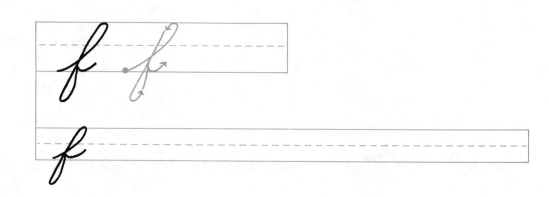

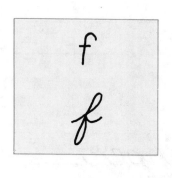

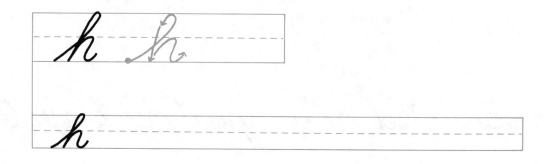

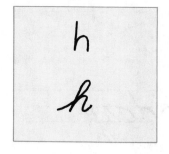

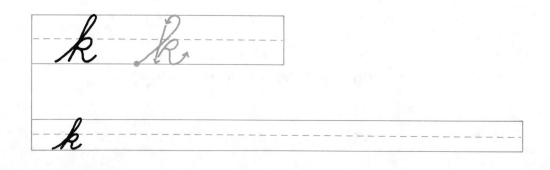

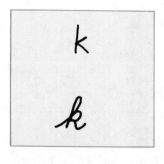

Practice: Copy the words.

leg line last mile sale sell tell

fun face feel fly if lift after

hand hat half he she they this

kiss kick kill ask like lake sky

Write these words: *like   half   feel   they   fly   sky*

Homework: Copy these phrases.

after class   after lunch

started a fire   first in line

has a key   high in the sky

a clean shirt   a pink skirt

Write these words: *life play fix hit shall take*

Homework: Copy these phrases.

half an apple   filled the glass

make a list   cheaper than this

feel fine   has a large kitchen

make a left turn   a dark night

Write these words: *three thirteen thirty third*

Homework: Copy these phrases.

a fine friend   in the fresh air

helped himself   a happy family

stuck in traffic   has dark hair

a little girl   in his right hand

Write these phrases: *feel sick   last night   eight fish*

Homework: Copy these phrases.

had fun   didn't learn anything

faster than the speed limit

laughs and makes a funny face

eat cake and drink milk

Write these phrases: *ask her*   *drink milk*   *thank them*

Lesson 5

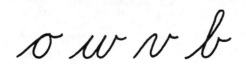

These letters *end* with a side-stroke like this: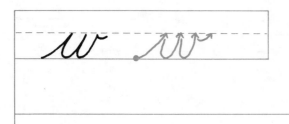

o
o

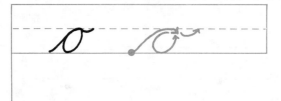

W
w

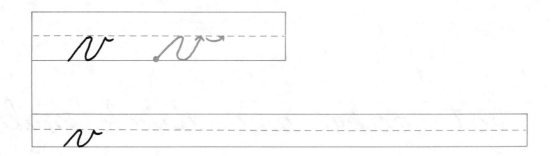

V
v

b
b

Practice: Copy these letters.

aw ew av iv ev ab eb ib ub

Copy these words.

do no so ago into radio zero

Copy these letters and words.

op open top ow show know

ou you four bu but burn

Write these words: go to stop snow you bus

Practice: Copy the letters and words.

oa coat road   wa was way

va van valley   ba bad bat

od today today   oc lock rock

bo boat boat   wo two two

Write these words: boat was van bad lock two

Practice: Copy the letters and words.

on one son on on some home

ox box oy boy by by baby

wh why ok look of of ob job

bl black blow ol old dollar

Write these words: *son some by boy old why*

Practice: Copy the letters and words.

be be bed bell we we went well

ve very have live oe does goes

bi big bill vi visit giving

wi wife will oi doing going

Write these words: be we will doing give giving

Practice: Copy the letters and words.

ot got hot not lot both other

or for more work door floor

br bring brother wr write

bs jobs ws blows os nose cost

Write these words: not for jobs bring work cost

Homework: Copy the words.

stop drop people know your but

load want wait bank o'clock

month don't from woman by

who what woke office table told

Write these words: *dollar old of look women one*

Homework: Copy the words.

best below were does over love

big with will doing driving

lot not mother or for store

broke brother knows most close

Write these words: be well will visit got color

Homework: Copy these phrases.

some people   costs five dollars

wear old clothes   don't forget

a baby boy   five below zero

baked potatoes save your money

Write these phrases: cold and windy   every woman

Homework: Copy these phrases.

two months ago   black coffee

come home   buy a loaf of bread

lock your door   got another job

go away   broken windows

Write this phrase: *have breakfast every morning*

Lesson 6

$C\ a\ \varepsilon$

These capital letters begin with a curve to the left:

c C
c C

C C
C

a A
a a

a a
a

e E
e ε

ε ε
ε

These capital letters begin with a curve to the left:

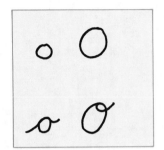

Practice: Connect C, A, and E to the next letter.

Do not connect O or Q to the next letter.

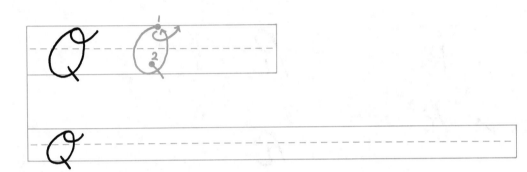

P R B

These capital letters begin like this:

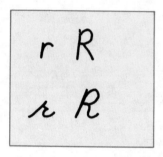

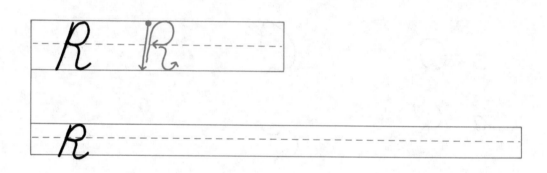

Practice: Connect R to the next letter, but do not connect P or B.

Ray Rose Robert Romano

Pam Pat Pete Bob Bud Bill

Copy these phrases.

Bill Porter and Pam Roberts

Pat Romano and Bob Black

Write these names: Rosa Parks   Robert Burns

T F

These capital letters begin with a top line like this:

t T
t T

f F
f F

Practice: Do not connect *T* or *F* to the next letter.

Ted Texas Tom Tony Ted

Fred Fran Friday Florida

Homework: Copy these sentences.

Carlos is from Cuba, not China.

Ann came to America in April.

Ellen is an English teacher.

Queen is the Oliver family's pup.

Write this sentence: *Canada can be cold in October.*

Homework: Copy these sentences.

Pam Porter married Bill Black.

Ray Roberts lives on River Road.

Tom takes the train to Texas.

Fran went to Florida on Friday.

Write this sentence: *Pat Romano visited Bob Fisher.*

Homework: Write these sentences.

Are you going to Canada in April?

Everyone had fun at Ed's party.

Robert Oliver pets his pup Queen.

Please phone Pete before Friday.

The Porters live in River City.

Queen Anne was an English queen.

This is the Fisher Office Building.

Both Carlos and Pablo speak English.

Lesson 7

N M K H

These capital letters begin like this: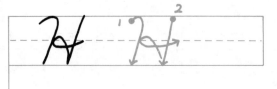

n N
n n

N *N*

n

m M
m M

M *M*

M

k K
k K

K *K*

K

h H
h H

H *H*

H

Practice: Connect N, M, and K to the next letter.

Ned Ned No No North Nurse

Mike Mr. Mrs. Miss Ms. May

Kim Kay Kitty King Keller

Connect H to the next letter by using a side-stroke.

Hugo Hope Mr. Hill Helen

Write these names: Mr. and Mrs. North   Helen Keller

ℒ 𝒟

These capital letters have a part like this:

I L	ℒ ℒ
l ℒ	ℒ

d D	𝒟 𝒟
d 𝒟	𝒟

Practice: Connect *L* to the next letter.

Lee Liz Lily Luther Lopez

Do not connect *D* to the next letter.

Dan Don Dr. Dad David

Homework: Copy these sentences.

Martin Luther King led a march.

Dr. King won the Nobel Peace Prize.

Helen Keller was blind and deaf.

Miss Keller learned to read Braille.

Write this sentence: *Kitty kissed Mother and Dad.*

Homework: Copy these sentences.

Maria's parents are from Mexico.

Maria was born in Dallas, Texas.

Liz lives at 45 North Hill Drive.

Hope was born on May 7, 1941.

Write this sentence: Dr. Lee can see you on March 18.

Homework: Write these sentences.

Mexico is in North America.

Ned fished in Nine Mile River.

Don hunted ducks in Mud Lake.

Let's ask Ms. Hill to go with us.

Nurse Mason works for Dr. Lopez.

Mr. and Mrs. Hunt live next door.

Labor Day is next Monday.

Kay and Ray Mason went camping.

Lesson 8

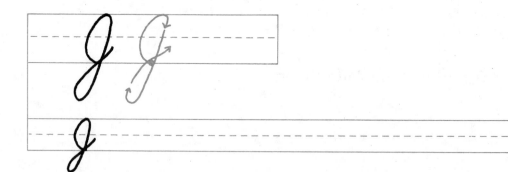

These capital letters begin like this:

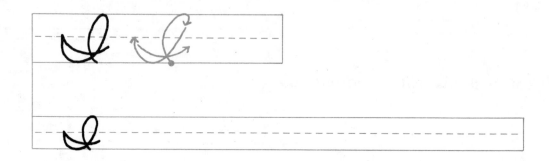

Practice: Connect *J* to the next letter.

Jill Jim Jane Jack John Jones

Connect *I* to the next letter by using a side-stroke.

Indian Indian I'm I'm I'll I'll

These capital letters begin like this:

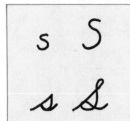

s S
s S

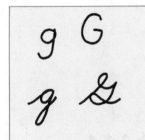

g G
g G

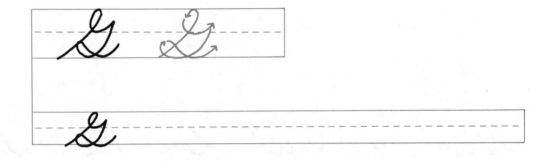

Practice: Connect S and G to the next letter.

Sam Steve Smith Street Stone

Gail Glenn Gray Green Garcia

Homework: Copy these sentences.

Shall I ask Gail to the party?

I'll see Joe Green next Saturday.

Give me Jack Smith's address.

Jill is at Green's Department Store.

Write this sentence: **Some states have Indian names.**

Homework: Write these sentences.

Gail and Jason Hunt are Jay's parents.

_____

Sam Garcia lives on Jones Street.

_____

Sometimes Glenn works on Saturday.

_____

Write a short No answer to each question.

Are you going home?   No, I am not.

Do you like rain?   _____

Have you eaten yet?   _____

Did you hear that?   _____

Do you have a boat?   _____

Are you ready?   _____

Have you finished?   _____

Lesson 9

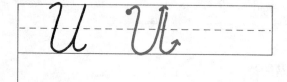

These capital letters begin with a curve like this: $\mathcal{C}$

| u U
 $\mathcal{u}$ $\mathcal{U}$ | $\mathcal{U}$ $\mathcal{U}$
 $\mathcal{U}$ |

| v V
 $\mathcal{v}$ $\mathcal{V}$ | $\mathcal{V}$ $\mathcal{V}$
 $\mathcal{V}$ |

| w W
 $\mathcal{w}$ $\mathcal{W}$ | $\mathcal{W}$ $\mathcal{W}$
 $\mathcal{W}$ |

| x X
 $\mathcal{x}$ $\mathcal{X}$ | $\mathcal{X}$ $\mathcal{X}$
 $\mathcal{X}$ |

Practice: Do not connect V or W to the next letter.

Van Valley Van Valley Van

Who What When Why We

Connect U and X to the next letter.

Uncle Union United University

Xavier Xavier Xavier Xavier

Write this sentence: *Where are Xavier and Uncle Van?*

Y Z

These capital letters end with a bottom loop:

Y Y
Y Y

Z Z
Z Z

Practice: Connect Y and Z to the next letter.

Yes Yes York York Young

Zion Zion Zion Zion Zion

Homework: Copy these sentences.

Mr. Young lives in Union City.

Van and I visited Zion Park.

Uncle Ned is in Washington.

Will went to Xavier University.

Write this sentence: *Van went to York University.*

Homework: Copy these sentences.

Mary White lives on York Street.

Van is in the Paper Workers Union.

We went to the Zion Church.

Where is Indian Valley?

Write this sentence: *You got a letter from Uncle Will.*

Homework: Answer each question with a sentence.

1. What is your name?

2. Where do you live?

3. When is your birthday?

4. Who is your teacher?

5. Were you in class yesterday?

6. Do you have a driver's license?

7. Have you finished your homework?

Lesson 10   **More Practice**

1. Write the letters.

a   b   c   d   e   f   g   h   i   j   k   l   m

n   o   p   q   r   s   t   u   v   w   x   y   z

2. Write the capital letters.

A   B   C   D   E   F   G   H   I

J   K   L   M   N   O   P   Q   R

S   T   U   V   W   X   Y   Z

3. Write the missing letters.

Read this note that a parent wrote to a teacher.

April 23, 1986

Dear Mrs. Gomez,
    My son John was not in school
last week because he was sick.
                    Ann Porter

Write this note to a teacher. Give today's date, and sign your own name.

Dear Mr. Smith,
    My son Ted was *not in school*
yesterday because he was *not*
feeling well.

1. Write this letter on the next page. Put today's date in the top right-hand corner. Sign your own name at the bottom.

(today's date)

Dear Uncle Lee,
   Thank you very much for the
clock radio. It wakes me up every
morning, and I listen to music
on it every evening. The rest of
the family is glad that the radio
came with an earphone!
   We hope that you are still
planning to visit us next
month. I look forward to
seeing you then.

Love,
(your name)

2. Address the envelope below to go with the letter. Write your own name and address in the top left-hand corner. Then address the envelope to:

Mr. Lee Jones
215 Peach Street
Selma, Alabama 36701

Read this check.

Pay to _Porter's Department Store_ $156.00
One hundred fifty-six and 00/100 ~~~ DOLLARS
March 15, 1986
Jason Hunt

Write a check to the York Music Shop for $45.86.
Give today's date, and sign your own name.

_____ 19 _____

Pay to _____ $ _____

_____ DOLLARS

_____

Write a check to Dr. Mary Washington for $215.00.

_____ 19 _____

Pay to _____ $ _____

_____ DOLLARS

_____